KUDOS for *Murder at the Estate Sale*

"Murder at the Estate Sale is erudite, suspenseful and simmering with sexual tension. Antiquarian booksellers Molly O'Donnell and Emma Clarke are lovable and believable sleuths. The book is an introduction to a fascinating world and a rip-roaring good time to read! I can't wait to see what Molly and Emma get into next."
-**Kate Jessica Raphael**, author of *Murder Under the Fig Tree* and *Murder Under the Bridge*

When I opened *Murder at the Estate Sale,* I expected to enter a familiar world of antiquarian booksellers, rare book fairs and estate sales, with a few dead bodies littering the bookshelves. That I did, but I also found a history of occult literature and a group of characters that make me wonder what my bookselling colleagues might be doing in the basement! There's a twist around every corner and a nice love story developing as well.
-**Lee Linn**, Bookseller
The Ridge Books, Calhoun, GA

"Lily Charles' *Murder at the Estate Sale* combines the bookish passion of A.S. Byatt's *Possession,* the occult history of Deborah Harkness' *A Discovery of Witches*, and the cozy mystery of Ellen Hart. Readers will love this peek behind the curtain of the rare book world and will cheer for the friendship and budding romance between likable amateur sleuths, Molly and Emma."
-**E.R. Anderson**, bookseller, Charis Books & More, Decatur, GA

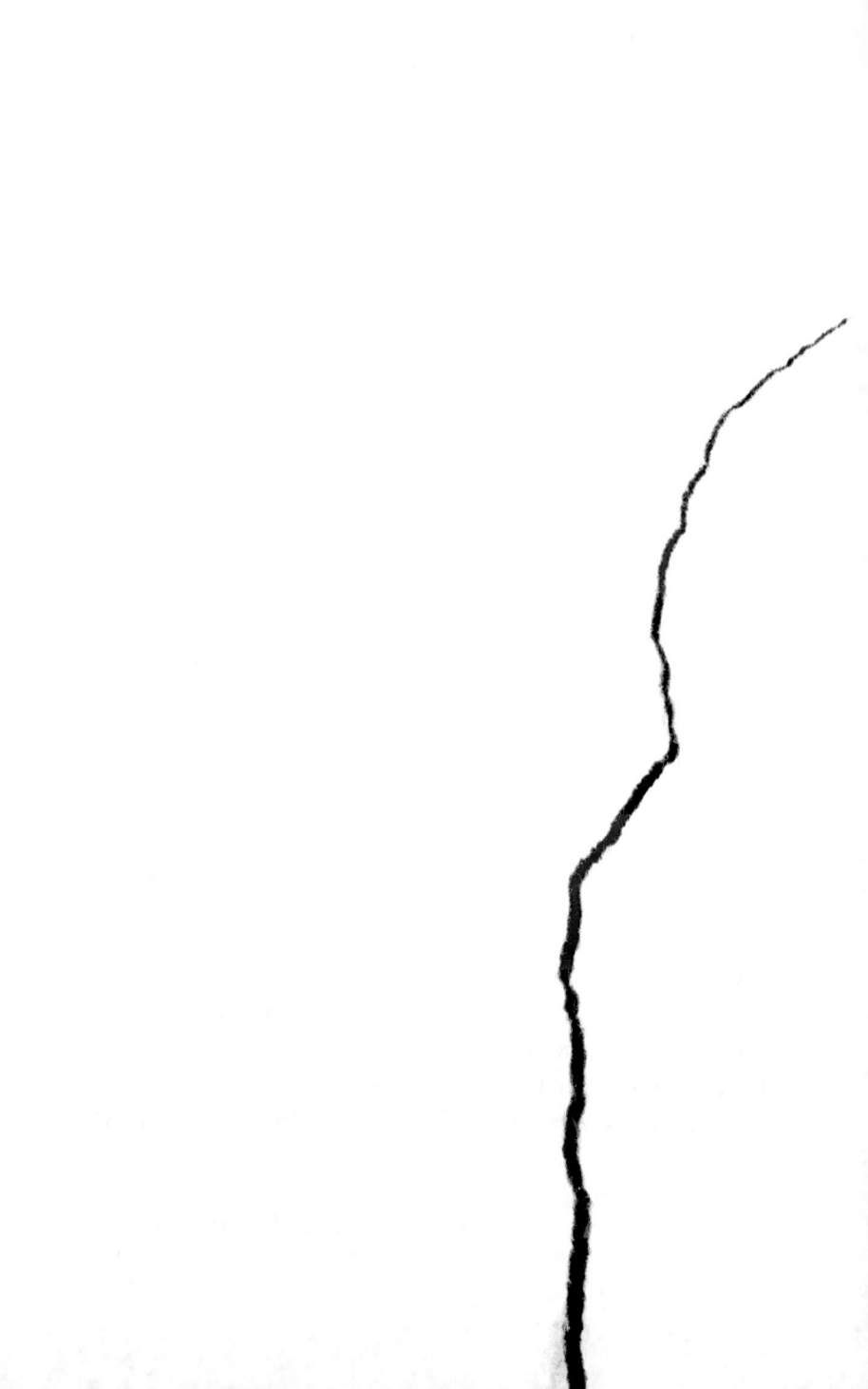

ACKNOWLEDGMENTS

First, we would like to thank our Writers' Group: Linda Bell, Valerie Fennell, Brenda Lloyd, and Maria Helena Dolan, for their encouragement and for many helpful suggestions. Many thanks also to Carol Lee Lorenzo for being an excellent writing coach, and to the members of the Tuesday morning writing workshop, especially Elizabeth Knowlton. We are grateful to Trudy Nan Boyce for her advice relating to police procedures. Thanks to Mary Dingee Fillmore for being our beta reader and for her insightful comments. Thanks to Laura Ownbey for editing the manuscript. And to our sister writers of Womonwrites, thank you for your enthusiastic encouragement.

Thanks to the Hambidge Center for the Arts and Sciences for the opportunity to write in a beautiful mountain setting—and great meals too! Thanks to Black Opal for their confidence in our book and to Susan Humphreys especially for her hard work in turning our manuscript into a finished product. Thanks to Caitlin Hamilton Summie and Rick Summie for publicity and marketing, and thanks to Caitlin for her infectious enthusiasm. Most of all, we would like to thank each other for being the best co-writer imaginable.

MURDER AT THE ESTATE SALE

First in the Molly & Emma Booksellers Series

Lily Charles

A Black Opal Books Publication

GENRE: BIBLIOMYSTERY/LGBTQ

This is a work of fiction. Names, places, characters and incidents are either the product of the author's imagination or are used fictitiously, and any resemblance to any actual persons, living or dead, businesses, organizations, events or locales is entirely coincidental. All trademarks, service marks, registered trademarks, and registered service marks are the property of their respective owners and are used herein for identification purposes only. The publisher does not have any control over or assume any responsibility for author or third-party websites or their contents. All books mentioned are real except *Against the Diabolical* and *The Boke of Secret Knowledge by a Learned Doctor*.

MURDER AT THE ESTATE SALE
Copyright © 2020 by Lily Charles
Cover Design by Transformational Concepts
Cover photos used with permission
All cover art copyright ©2020
All Rights Reserved
Print ISBN: 9781644372449

First Publication: AUGUST 2020

All rights reserved under the International and Pan-American Copyright Conventions. No part of this book may be reproduced or transmitted in any form or by any means, electronic or mechanical, including photocopying, recording, or by any information storage and retrieval system, without permission in writing from the publisher.

WARNING: The unauthorized reproduction or distribution of this copyrighted work is illegal. Criminal copyright infringement, including infringement without monetary gain, is investigated by the FBI and is punishable by up to 5 years in federal prison and a fine of $250,000. Anyone pirating our eBooks will be prosecuted to the fullest extent of the law and may be liable for each individual download resulting therefrom.

ABOUT THE PRINT VERSION: If you purchased a print version of this book without a cover, you should be aware that the book is stolen property. It was reported as "unsold and destroyed" to the publisher, and neither the author nor the publisher has received any payment for this "stripped book."

IF YOU FIND AN EBOOK OR PRINT VERSION OF THIS BOOK BEING SOLD OR SHARED ILLEGALLY, PLEASE REPORT IT TO:
skh@blackopalbooks.com

Published by Black Opal Books **http://www.blackopalbooks.com**

DEDICATION

Dedicated to all booksellers everywhere

CHAPTER 1
Steep Stairs

Arthur Edward Waite, The Brotherhood of the Rosy Cross, *1924, red with gilt Rosy Cross on cover, spine with gilt lettering, sixteen full-page plates. History and discussion of Rosicrucianism, alchemy, symbolism, and myth.*

Molly wasn't a morning person, not by a long shot, but for a book sale, she could jump out of bed before the dew dried. The announcement had read, "Estate sale of nonagenarian, tons of books including children's, cookbooks, leather, and a signed first edition of *Gone with the Wind*." Molly knew that antique dealers as well as book dealers would be lining up for *Gone with the Wind*. Not her, though: she'd be checking out the rest of the tonnage. And she'd had good luck in the Sherwood Forest area of Atlanta.

As soon as she turned onto Friar Tuck Way, she saw a line of vans pulled up along the street. *Please let me be in the first twenty-five,* she wished. The women who ran these estate sales only let twenty-five people in at a time. Since Scott's Antique Market was this weekend, more dealers than usual were in town.

Hurrying down the driveway in front of the yellow brick ranch house, she saw a knot of dealers. *The usual suspects*, she thought, walking up behind Harry and Jay, two dealers she'd known for years. "Hi, guys."

"Molly!" Jay exclaimed, bouncing from one foot to the other. He beamed, his reddish hair standing on end. Never still, he reminded Molly of a squirrel in the road.

Harry stooped to put an arm around Molly in a lazy embrace. She had to stretch up to hug his bulky shoulders. He wore a thin, faded black T-shirt, and his graying ponytail was pulled back with an elastic band with a turquoise and silver ornament. Harry and Jay owned a store together: Blind Tiger Books.

Jay was exclaiming over his latest sale. "I paid a hundred bucks for an Andy Warhol broadside, bidding at 4:00 a.m. on eBay, and sold it recently for twenty-five hundred."

Molly counted the people in front of her. "Who's ahead of me?"

"Me," said a dealer standing by Jay. "And I'm after him." He pointed to Harry.

Good, she thought. *I'm eleventh in line, not too far behind Harry and Jay.*

A short, dark-haired woman came down the walk, pulling a rolling cart behind her. Molly remembered seeing her at the St. Pete book fair. Then she groaned. Buck Hubbell, wearing a wide-shouldered, tan travel jacket and carrying several tote bags, trotted behind the woman, trying to overtake her so he'd be ahead in line.

As the woman came up behind her, Molly said, "Hi. I'm Molly. I think we met in St. Pete, but I don't remember your name." She put out her hand, and the woman shook it, her hand cold as a Creamsicle.

"Emma Clarke." She dropped Molly's hand and quickly stepped sideways closer to Molly, pulling her rolling cart in front of her and thus cutting off Buck, who had tried to push between them. He scowled and stood close behind Emma, clutching his empty tote bags.

"Hmmpf," he said to no one in particular, sniffing. "I smell dog."

Molly ignored him. He didn't have much room to talk, considering that he reeked of garlic and onions as if his sweat glands were working overtime.

She turned her attention back to Emma. Female sellers were rare, so she was happy to meet her. "St. Pete your first book fair?"

"Yes. I've been collecting for years, and after looking around my house and deciding that they were taking over, I decided it was time to make room—for more books."

Molly laughed. "I think a lot of us start out as collectors."

Buck wandered to the house to look in the windows. Molly said in an undertone, "Watch out for that guy, he's a known book thief."

"A book thief?"

Molly nodded. "Buck Hubbell. I call him Bucky Burglar. He's a pain at library sales. He'll dig under tables when it's not allowed, and I've seen him go behind bookstore counters. In fact, he's been banned from some of Atlanta's finest bookstores."

"Why don't they ban him from estate sales?"

"People that run estate sales don't necessarily know about what goes on in the world of bookselling. It's a totally different world."

More people were arriving: retired couples who sold antiques as a hobby, book scouts who would sell their finds to bookstores, owners of antique stores, dealers who traveled to antique fairs, and curious neighbors of the ninety-year-old book collector.

Two elderly women arrived in a vintage Cadillac.

Joyce, in an ivory pantsuit, helped Maisie out of the car and got her walker from the back. Maisie, gleaming white hair in a pixie cut and wearing a brocade pink jacket and long, pink crepe skirt, proceeded slowly towards the house. The dealers in line drew back to let the women pass.

"Need help?" asked a man in a tweed jacket who stood by the door. Michael was an engineer who frequented the sales.

"Naw, I'm fine," drawled Maisie. "Seems like I been like this forever, but I keep on goin'." But she accepted his elbow, let him take the walker, and leaned on him to go up the three steps. She disappeared into the house behind her walker.

"That's Joyce and Maisie, who run these estate sales," murmured Molly to Emma.

"I'm new to estate sales. How do they work?"

"Well, you have to stand in line in the order you arrived. Everyone here knows that and will tell you to move back if you try to get in ahead of them. When the door opens precisely at ten o'clock, they let in twenty-five people at a time and then shut the door."

"Do they ever let anyone in early?"

"Never! Not even in snow and sleet. Once you get in, make a mad dash to where the books are. They may be all over the house, or in the library, the basement, or upstairs. If you see something you think you want, don't hesitate. Grab first, examine later. That's why it's good to bring lots of tote bags."

Emma nodded. "What kind of books are you interested in?"

"Occult, cookbooks, books about books, illustrated."

"Occult? That's astrology, witchcraft, stuff like that?" Emma raised an eyebrow.

"Right. Also spiritualism. I've got some Blavatsky, Annie Besant, and a beautiful illustrated volume on

Rosicrucians by Arthur Waite. I even named one of my dogs Blavatsky." Emma frowned. Molly wondered if it was because of Molly's interest in occult or in reaction to the mention of a dog. "What do you sell?"

"Children's, a few illustrated classics. So I overlap with you a bit."

The door opened, and dealers started to file in, Molly and Emma among them. Maisie sat at a small table inside, counting them as they passed.

"Books?" Molly asked.

"Thirteen, to the left, and everywhere, fourteen, fifteen."

Buck pushed past them both. Molly noticed that Emma stayed close behind her as she ran into the large library on the left. *I hope she doesn't stick to me like a burr,* Molly thought. Making new friends was all very well, but once inside, it was everyone for herself. Other dealers were already pulling books off the ceiling-high shelves and stuffing them into their tote bags. Some had brought rolling carts, like Emma. Others created piles on the floor. Molly planted herself in front of a shelf and began filling her bags. Later she would check to see if they were first editions or signed.

Out of the corner of her eye, she saw Emma kneeling at a low shelf and stuffing books into a large bag in her rolling cart, dark, gray-streaked hair screening her face. *She's cute,* thought Molly. Then she scolded herself: *she's probably straight, with those shoes*. Emma wore thin-soled ballet-type flats. Molly glanced down at her own all-terrain sandals with satisfaction. She saw a *Mockingbird* and drew in her breath. It was a first edition book club. Had a picture of the author on the back—photo by Truman Capote. She stuffed it into her bag. Quickly she scanned titles before anyone else invaded her section of the built-in shelves. She decided to look for cookbooks. Most of these older homes had a copy of *Mrs. Dull's Southern Cooking*, a book she could always sell.

She stepped into the hallway, looking for more bookshelves, when she noticed a door, slightly ajar, with a sign reading: "Do Not Enter." She felt a moment's impulse to open it a little more and take a peek. But Jay trotted down the hall, his backpack bulging, so she turned away from the door. She started in the direction of the kitchen, intent on cookbooks, when she heard a muffled scream.

Molly jerked her head up as Emma Clarke burst through the door and collided with her. Molly gently disentangled herself from Emma, who seemed distraught. "What's the matter? You look like you've seen a ghost."

Emma shook her head. "No—not a ghost. The real thing—maybe someone's dead—come look!"

"Someone's dead!?"

"Come on!"

The door led, as Molly had suspected, down to the basement. The steps were steep and not quite wide enough for the length of a foot. A bare bulb at the foot of the stairs gave a dim light. She followed Emma carefully, placing her sandals sideways and feeling with her hand on the rough framing and drywall, as there was no rail.

Molly reached the bottom of the stairs, took in a breath, and widened her eyes. She saw in front of her a floor to ceiling wall of shelves, full of books. "Wow," she said under her breath.

"Look!" Emma urged, tugging at her sleeve.

Molly glanced down and gasped.

A man lay crumpled on the floor, a few feet away from the stairs, right in front of the shelves. On his back, he lay very still. His tan travel jacket was open, revealing many inside pockets, all filled with books. Books were spilling out of bags and more were scattered about. A dark pool was spreading out from under his head. Some of the books had been spattered.

"Oh, my god," whispered Molly. "It's Buck Hubbell!"

Emma nodded, pressing her hand over her mouth. She was breathing hard.

Molly's first impulse was to rush to rescue the books from the dreadful, spreading puddle. With another part of her mind, she noticed that the basement was finished, with a concrete floor, that the shelves were metal and the books looked old, and that the air was not as damp as one might expect in a basement. *Dehumidifier,* she thought. *This is a serious book-storage place.*

"Do you think he's, uh, still alive?" asked Emma, bringing her hand down from her mouth. "Should we check?"

Molly drew a deep breath and carefully stepped over the books, picking up some and putting them out of reach of the puddle. She pushed away other items scattered on the floor—a cellphone, a notepad, a pen—and squatted down next to the motionless man. She hesitated and lifted his outstretched hand. It was limp but still warm. She turned it over and placed the first two fingers of her left hand where his pulse should be. After a moment, she shook her head. "I don't feel any pulse." She thought, *Oh, my god, all the times I had bad thoughts about him, and now he's dead.* She looked up. "What happened? I mean, how did you—" She couldn't think of how to ask, *what were you doing in the basement when the sign on the door clearly read "Do Not Enter"?*

"I was in the hallway, and I heard what sounded like voices, people arguing. They seemed to be coming from behind the door. It was ajar, so I stopped to listen. At that moment, I heard a loud thud, and one of the voices went, 'Uhhh!' I pulled the door open and stepped down a few steps—the light was on—and I thought I heard footsteps. Then nothing. I called, 'Is anything wrong?' I looked around and saw—him—lying on the floor."

Molly looked at her, eyes wide. "You just heard someone killing Buck."

They stared at one another. Then, as though on cue, they both glanced around. Molly had a chilling thought: *could the killer still be here?*

No sound or movement. Pulling out their phones, they simultaneously dialed 911, but neither could get a signal. "That's odd," Emma said.

"We better tell Joyce and Maisie." Molly started to get to her feet, but stopped. "Look. What's that?" She pointed to a small, yellowed piece of paper that lay next to the man's leg.

"Does it matter right now?" whispered Emma.

"I don't know," Molly said. "But—" She reached with care across the motionless figure on the floor, avoiding the puddle and the books, and carefully picked up the paper by one corner.

"We probably shouldn't touch anything."

Molly squinted, reading aloud slowly, "*Whosoever readeth this boke without leave of the Circle, let him BEWARE. SF.*" She stood up, knees creaking. "Look, 'BEWARE' is in all caps, and the initials are written extra large." She held out the fragile paper for Emma to see.

Emma peered at it. "Looks like Elizabethan or Jacobean script." She touched the other woman's shoulder. "Molly, please! Let's go tell someone."

Molly glanced around her, the paper in her fingers. Her heart wrenched at the sight of the blood-stained, splayed, crumpled volumes at her feet. She started to pick her way towards the stairs, but stopped when a disembodied, deep Southern drawl uttered, "No one is allowed down heah."

They both jumped, and Emma gave a small shriek. "Help! Someone's—hurt."

Molly looked up toward the top of the stairs and saw

Joyce in the doorway. "Joyce, call the police!" she yelled. As she spoke, she carefully slipped the paper into her tote bag and pushed it behind her.

"Wha-at?" said Joyce.

Emma said, "I think he's dead."

"What?" Joyce repeated. "Y'all come back up heah." As they climbed the stairs, she stepped back just enough to let them through the door, then shut it firmly.

In the hallway, Molly tried her cell phone again. This time it worked. As she dialed 911, she heard Joyce say, "If people would just follow directions, things like this wouldn't happen."

CHAPTER 2
Dr. Tooth

Sarah Stanley Grimke, Esoteric Lessons, *1900, grey cloth with black lettering on spine and front cover. Spiritual philosophy.*

Molly and Emma stood outside, watching the other dealers milling about in the driveway and on the lawn. Molly heard the name of Buck coming from more than one group as people told stories about the dead man. The 911 dispatcher had told Molly that everyone should stay until officers got there. When two detectives arrived, they went up to people and began asking questions. An ambulance had also arrived with paramedics followed by the medical examiner, who pronounced Buck dead.

"Ms. O'Donnell?" The voice was so low she thought for a minute it was a man, but it came from a woman in street clothes who had quietly walked up to her. "I'm Detective DuBois. Are you Molly O'Donnell?"

"Yes," Molly said.

Detective DuBois had short-cropped brown hair with random grey strands sticking straight up. *Ha,* thought Molly. *She's pulling out the grey ones.* She knew from experience what happened when plucked hairs grew back in.

"Did you know the deceased, Buckminster Hubbell?"

Molly hid a smile. *So that's Buck's real name. No wonder he went by Buck.* "Yes, officer. He's—he was—a well-known book collector."

She told Detective DuBois she had not seen Buck go downstairs, that she had just met Emma Clarke, that she had gone to the basement because Emma urged her to go downstairs. "I did take his pulse."

"If we need more from you, we'll be in touch," said Detective DuBois. "Are you planning on leaving town?"

"No."

"Well, if you do, please let us know. Here's my card. And call if you remember anything else."

"I will." *Am I a suspect?* she wondered.

Molly went over to where Emma was standing, hands clasped, rubbing her knuckles with her thumb.

"What did they ask you?" Emma asked.

Molly told her.

Emma nodded. "Same for me."

But not exactly the same, Molly thought. *You found him.* For a moment, she wondered if there was more that Emma hadn't told her.

Detective DuBois stepped up onto the stoop and called for everyone's attention. "The estate sale has been cancelled," she announced. "You must leave your purchases here. You can return next week and pick them up."

The dealers exploded. "What do you mean, we have to leave our stuff here?" said Jay.

"You can come back next Friday," said Joyce, holding her hands in a placating clasp. "We'll have the sale then."

"I can't come back next Friday!" shouted one dealer. "I'm from Ohio. I'm just here for the Scott Antique Show. Next week I'll be in Pennsylvania."

"How do we know our stuff will still be here?" yelled another.

Maisie said, "Write your name and phone number on a sticky and put it on your pile. We'll make sure it's safe."

Emma sighed. "So I guess we won't get to look over our spoils."

"Let's go grab a cup of coffee and talk about it," Molly said.

A sleek black BMW convertible careened around the corner and roared to a stop in front of the house. The license plate read: "DRTOOTH." The driver, a balding man with a few strands stretching across his scalp, jumped out and ran toward Maisie. "What the—!" he bellowed. "I told you to keep that basement door locked. Those stairs are dangerous."

"It *was* locked," Maisie said, turning, one hand on her walker and the other on the car door handle.

"I was about to replace a goddam filling—"

Joyce came up behind the man and said firmly without raising her voice, "Theah is no need for that kind of language, Dr. Booth."

His face turned red. No member of the Southern elite could continue yelling after such a graceful rebuke.

"I better go check that lock," he muttered.

But Detective DuBois stepped forward. "Sir, this is a crime scene. No one is allowed in the house."

"But it's my house now!"

She spoke into a box on her shoulder, and the young male officer approached the doctor. "I'll escort you inside, Dr. Tooth."

"It's Booth!" he snapped.

"I bet he gets that a lot," Molly muttered to Emma.

Detective DuBois said, "You all move along now."

People slowly walked back to their vehicles, parting so Joyce and Maisie could back the Cadillac out.

Molly raised her eyebrows to Emma. "How about that coffee?"

Emma looked at her watch. "Is it too early for a drink?"

CHAPTER 3
Planning in Oxygen

Arthur Edward Waite, The Book of Ceremonial Magic. The Secret Tradition in Goetia; Including the Rites and Mysteries of Goetic Theurgy, Sorcery and Infernal Necromancy, *1911, white cloth with gilt on spine and top of pages. Cover has Magician from the Waite/Rider tarot deck in gilt. History of ceremonial magic by one of the leaders of the Golden Dawn. Part II is a grimoire.*

Sitting in Oxygen, a popular coffee shop that became a bar at night, Emma sipped a glass of pinot noir, feeling the wine's warmth spread out from her chest. Her breath was coming slowly now, thanks to the wine and the blessed ordinariness of sitting across the table with this matter-of-fact, capable-looking woman with a T-shirt that read "I Sleep with Books." Emma imagined Molly in a wide bed, half of it covered with books, Molly's arm thrown possessively over them.

Molly leaned forward, elbows on the table. "If I'm right, that note is old, *really* old."

Emma sighed. "Molly, you shouldn't have taken that piece of paper. You should have given it to the police. It might be important."

"I'm not sure myself why I didn't tell about the note." Molly pulled out the yellowed piece of old paper from her large tote bag. "I only know that I have to examine it more carefully. I'm curious about what book it fell out of. If I give the note to the police, it'll never be matched with the one it came from."

"So?"

Molly frowned. "You don't separate laid-in ephemera from their books. It's one of the rules of bookselling."

"Ephemera?"

"You know, something not meant to last. Notes, letters, bookmarks, brochures."

"But if you keep it, you're tampering with evidence!" insisted Emma. "It could be important to the police in investigating what—what happened to Buck."

"Why he was murdered." Molly looked grim.

Emma drew in her breath. "You don't think it was an accident?"

Molly shook her head. "I got a close look at him. All that damage didn't come from hitting his head on the floor, even a concrete floor. Somebody bashed the back of his head."

"But why are you so obsessed with that note?"

Molly leaned forward. "Those books on that shelf I was looking at? Before Joyce interrupted me? I think at least one of them might be a grimoire."

"Grim-wa?" Emma frowned. "What's that?"

"A book of magic spells. Like for summoning demons."

"Demons? You *are* kidding, right?"

"No, I'm not," Molly said in a low voice. "There were lots of occult books. Old ones. Why weren't those books in the basement part of the sale?"

"There could be lots of reasons. Maybe that dentist wanted to keep them for himself." She shrugged. "Maybe *he's* into black magic."

Molly gave her a considering look. "I have to go back and look at those books. That note must have come out of one of them. I need to see which one."

Emma narrowed her eyes. "Why? Are *you* into black magic?" She had noticed Molly's pendant, with what looked like a magician on a blue background.

"No," Molly said in a firm voice. "But I do collect occult books."

"Do you own any of those—grimoires?"

"No." Molly shook her head. "I once bought one, called *The Goetia*. It was handwritten and hand sewn. Thick, handmade paper, leather cover. It was full of symbols for ritual magic. Totally unreadable for the uninitiated. Took it to the Scott Antique Market, and this odd, pale young man came up to look at it. He studied it a long time and then said he was going to go ask his master if he wanted him to buy it."

Emma drew in a breath.

Molly continued, "He went away, came back, and bought the book. I never saw who he bought it for. I never bought a grimoire again."

"Different strokes? S/M with a little black magic thrown in?"

Molly shrugged. "I don't think he was that kind of master. I felt creepy about the book." She sipped her carmelatto. It left a bit of foam on her upper lip.

Emma looked carefully at Molly. Her eyes lingered a moment on the fleck of foam. She took another sip of pinot noir.

A look of resolve tightened Molly's mouth. "I'm going back to look at those books."

"You mean you're going back next week when Joyce and Maisie open the house again to finish the estate sale? I hope that's what you mean."

"No, I'm going back before then. I'm going to get into that basement."

"No!" burst out Emma. The young woman at the next table gave them a glance. Emma lowered her voice to a whisper. "That's breaking and entering. You'd be interfering with a crime scene. You might damage evidence. No telling what might happen. It's illegal!"

Molly nodded. "That's right. Want to come?"

Chapter 4
Breaking and Entering

Israel Regardie, Foundations of Practical Magic: An Introduction to Qabalistic, Magic and Meditative Techniques, *1979, blue cloth with gilt lettering on spine, illustrated dust jacket. By Aleister Crowley's secretary and biographer, this book includes a Qabalistic primer and practical methods of healing, meditation, and using magic.*

As Molly parked her van in front of Oxygen, she saw Emma sitting at a sidewalk table wearing black capri leggings under a short black knit dress.

Molly erupted in laughter. "You look like a ninja."

"I'm going more for the black cat look," Emma said with a wry smile.

"Like Catwoman in *Batman* or cat burglar in *To Catch a Thief*?"

"Hmm. Eartha Kitt or Cary Grant? Both attractive, don't you think?"

Is she trying to signal that she's bi? Or that she gets the pop culture and movie allusions? Molly laughed again. "Well, I didn't wear a costume or my best clothes. Jeans and T-shirts won't call attention to themselves." Her faded blue T-shirt read: "I brake for bookstores."

"Oh, Molly, I don't know about this." A crease deepened between Emma's dark eyebrows.

"It'll be fine," Molly said. "There's got to be a way to get into that basement that doesn't constitute breaking and entering. Someone got in and out quickly, so it's probably unlocked."

"It would still be interfering with a crime scene."

Molly wondered if she should have invited Emma. What if they did need to bend the law a little? "Let's get going. Wanna go in my van?"

They rode in silence from Grant Park north to Sherwood Forest through the dusk of a late summer evening. Molly had a thousand questions she wanted to ask—about Emma's past, her business, her likes. Did she like old movies? Hitchcock? But most importantly, why did she agree to go on such a venture with someone she just met, especially as she wasn't interested in occult books? But she did discover the body.

Molly rolled down the window and heard the summer sound of cicadas as the night descended. Most of the Sherwood Forest homes were simple ranches, but being in this neighborhood pushed their values into the two million dollar range. She pulled her van to the edge of a small park with a deep ravine that cut the neighborhood in two. Trails ran along the edge of a stream at the bottom. One afternoon, she had brought her dogs here for a run, so she knew it wouldn't look odd if a car were seen parked here.

"The Booth house is over there on the other street." Molly pointed. "We can go through the backyards in case the police have anyone guarding it."

"Backyards?" Emma looked worried. "Hope no gun

nuts see us."

"You're such an optimist. But you won't get hit, you'll look like a shadow."

"So if you get shot, I'll fall down, too."

Molly said, "You had the right idea dressing in black. For my next adventure, I think I will too."

Emma shot her a look through narrowed lids. "*Next* adventure?"

"You're as curious as I am," Molly said with a grin. "Admit it."

In the darkness, they quietly slipped across a backyard behind the Booth house. A wild hedge separated the two lots. They found a gap to squeeze through.

As Molly had suspected, the Booth house was surrounded by yellow tape. They made their way slowly through tall grasses and vines with only the light of the rising full moon. The backyard of the Booth house seemed more like a field that no one had mown since well before the death of Dr. Booth's grandfather.

"Oh!" muttered Emma. "I nearly tripped."

"Shhh!" whispered Molly.

"There's a pile of bricks or stones there," returned Emma. "Be careful."

Molly held back an expletive as her toe hit a hard object. Feeling with her fingers, she encountered what felt like crumbling brick. "It's an old foundation or something."

"There may have been an older house on this site," Emma said. "I read an article about a farmhouse in this area."

Approaching the house, Molly noticed a detached building at the end of the driveway that looked like a two-story garage with an apartment. Unusual for a ranch house. That would argue for another house once being on this lot. As they moved closer to the back of the brick house, she stopped short. "Where's the back door?" she whispered.

"Don't see one," Emma whispered back.

"These 1950's ranch houses usually have full basements with a back door to the basement," murmured Molly. "Doesn't look as though there's a side door either."

"This looks harder than we thought," Emma whispered. "But whoever did it got out somehow."

Molly moved slowly along the back side of the house, feeling the rough brick surface. "Maybe it's hidden."

"Molly, how can you hide a door in brick?"

"Let's think. If you had a secret basement, how would you get in?"

"Through the inside of the house?"

Molly tapped her fingers on her lips. Suddenly a car pulled into the driveway, headlights blazing.

"Oh, no!" Emma burst out. She grabbed Molly's arm and pulled her against the back wall of the house where they both crouched, panting. A moment later, car doors slammed. The garage, casting a dark shadow, loomed not ten feet from them. Emma whispered, "Let's run and hide behind the garage."

Running, crouched over, they ducked behind the garage just as two neighborhood watch guards, recognizable by their yellow vests, rounded the corner of the house, laughing.

"Your aunt? When was this?"

"I was seventeen, and she was thirty-eight."

"Oh, man!"

"So I saw her at my cousin's wedding. Fifty-two and still hot."

"Did you—" The voice faded into the darkness.

Molly felt something hard pressing against her back. Reaching around, she found a doorknob. Not wanting to leave fingerprints, she covered her hand with the end of her T-shirt and turned it. To her surprise, the door started to open inward. Trying not to make any sound, she eased backwards into the dark garage, and Emma slipped in after her.

CHAPTER 5

The Secret Room

Heinrich Cornelius Agrippa, The Philosophy of Natural Magic, *1913, red cloth with gilt on spine and front cover. Detailed study of white magic and black magic.*

Molly pulled the door shut. Silence. Musty smells. She pulled out her slender flashlight and lit a tiny area of the floor, holding her hand over it to minimize its glow.

"Careful," Emma whispered. "They might see it through the door."

"I'll keep it covered like this." Molly cast the tiny beam back and forth over the floor. They could see that they were in a small room full of boxes of various sizes.

"Wonder if this stuff was kept from the estate sale," Molly murmured. She pulled open one of the boxes and revealed a tangle of Christmas lights. "Uh-huh. I see why."

As Molly swept her light around, Emma noticed rickety steps leading upward, and a little door under them. "Look!" she whispered,"The famous cupboard under the stairs." She'd read all the Harry Potters.

"At number four, Privet Drive," added Molly with a giggle.

Tiptoeing over to the door, Molly tried the knob. It turned. She carefully pulled the door open, trying not to make any sound. It did not creak, and it pulled open easily, as though it were often used.

"Anything in there?" whispered Emma. "Owl feathers? Wands?"

Molly moved her tiny beam of light around the dark space, revealing narrow steps leading downward and out of sight.

Emma peered down. "A basement under a garage?"

"Let's see what's down there!" whispered Molly. "You game?"

Emma took a deep breath. "Sure."

They slipped through the tiny door, Molly first with the darting flashlight. Emma pulled the door closed behind them, and they began to edge their way down the narrow steps. They felt surprisingly sturdy under her feet. No wobbling, no unsteadiness. Seeing by the light of Molly's flashlight, Emma noticed that new boards had been nailed in on a couple of the steps. These stairs, although old based on their width, were being maintained.

Emma's foot slipped, and she clutched at the fabric of Molly's T-shirt. Molly stopped a moment as though surprised, then went on. Emma could feel the back of the other woman's bra under the shirt that covered her warm, wide back, and she held on, even though she didn't really need to, as they crept downward.

Molly stopped, and Emma collided with her, nose against clean hair smell, tickled by short neck curls. She let go of Molly's shirt. They had reached the bottom of the stairs. Molly swept the tiny flashlight from side to side, revealing a narrow passageway barely tall enough for them to stand up in without stooping.

"Okay, here we go," Molly whispered and started along the passage. Its floor was brick, and its walls were irregular stone.

"This has been here a while," whispered Emma.

"Uh-huh. At least as long as this house. Maybe longer."

Emma's first impression was that the passage smelled of damp earth. They were under the backyard, after all. The idea was not pleasant. She had a touch of claustrophobia and tried not to think of all the Georgia clay piled up over her head. To shut out that image, she began to wonder how old the passage was. What if it *did* predate the house? Sherwood Forest was fairly new, as Atlanta neighborhoods went—from the 1950's and 60's. She thought of the article about the old farmhouse. Could this be it? Where had the tunnel once led? To a basement for canning and keeping produce and meat? Why not a simple basement?

The passage had come to an end, and facing them in the darting light of the flashlight was a door. A fairly modern-looking metal door. Molly gave it a push, and the door swung inward. Stepping carefully inside, she cast her flashlight's beam around.

"Oh, my goodness," breathed Emma. Her eyes followed the light around a room with flat paving stones for flooring. A chill seemed to pervade the space and settle around them. On the floor was a faded circle drawn in what looked like chalk. Within the circle appeared a five-sided star and roughly scrawled, foreign-looking words and symbols. A plain, long, wooden table stood between two points of the pentagram. Puddles of white candle wax were at each corner of the table.

"Well, well, well," Molly said. "So Grandpa Booth was into dark magic."

"How do you know it's dark?"

"For black magic rituals, the head of the pentagram is between two points, like the devil's horns."

Emma shuddered.

"And this space has been used not too long ago," went on Molly. "Look how clean the room is: no cobwebs, no debris, no sign of rats."

"Please stop talking about rats," said Emma. She had a flash of memory that ran through her veins like ice. "Molly! I just remembered. I forgot to say it before. But…when I started down the basement stairs, right before I saw Buck's body… I thought I saw the bookshelf move."

"Umm?" Molly said absently, examining the table. She crouched and peered under it.

"Molly! Listen to me," Emma said with urgency. "It may be important. As I started down the stairs, right before I saw the body, I thought I saw the bookshelf move. The part on my left. It seemed to shift, turn just a tiny bit."

"What?" Molly straightened up, now all attention.

"I didn't say anything to the police. I thought I imagined it. Then I forgot because of—everything else we were all focused on."

"So—?" Molly's voice held a hint of impatience. "What are you saying?"

"The bookshelves." Emma felt her words were tumbling over each other, trying to come out. "That's—that's how the person who killed Buck got out of the basement! There must be a door in the bookshelf. I mean, one of the shelves is a door."

Molly's eyes widened. She looked around the room. Six stone archways formed its sides, brick filling in the archway of all but one, which contained a rectangular outline that looked like a door frame. She took out a handkerchief and pressed on it. Suddenly a click sounded, loud as a gunshot to Emma. She jumped with a small cry.

The panel began to open. They both watched, fascinated, as the wall swung into the room with the bookshelves where they had discovered the body.

"Speak, friend, and enter," murmured Molly. She waited until the door had stopped moving, and stepped resolutely through it.

CHAPTER 6
Vellum, Manuscripts, and Witches, Oh, My!

Reginald Scot, The Discoverie of Witchcraft, *1930, green cloth with leather spine, untrimmed pages. Facsimile of 1584 first edition, limited edition of 1,275. Scot's refutation of the existence of witches and his argument that the poor and old should not be persecuted as witches.*

"It's not like in the movies," Molly whispered. "There's no chalk outline." She felt a chill that had nothing to do with the temperature as she looked at the concrete floor where the crumpled body of Buck had lain. Could you feel the presence of death where someone had recently been killed? She rubbed her goose-bumped arms, wishing she had brought her jacket. *Poor Buck*, she found herself thinking.

Carefully stepping around the area as though an invisible body lay there, they faced the bookshelves. Molly remembered how cold the basement had been earlier. But not damp. This space was climate-controlled like a library. She started to reach for the pull cord.

"Wait." Emma touched Molly's arm. "Don't turn on the light. Somebody might see it. This is a crime scene.

We shouldn't—"

"I won't mess up anything," Molly said. The light, warm hand on her forearm fell away.

Emma followed her. "Molly, we shouldn't move or touch anything. Oh, why did I let you talk me into this?"

Molly turned, suddenly annoyed. "Talk you into? I said do you want to come, and you said—"

"Yes," came out in a faint voice. "I said 'yes.' I was caught up in the moment."

Molly's annoyance evaporated. "Don't quit on me now," she said, touching Emma's shoulder. "We won't turn on the light, and I'll be careful. Look. One hand behind my back. The other hand will hold the flashlight. No hands free to touch any evidence."

"What if those guards come in here?"

"They're only neighborhood watch. They're not supposed to go inside houses. And we'll be very quiet." She took a step closer to the shelves, holding the flashlight up to the row at eye level and moving it side to side. A faint odor of old books reached her nostrils and she inhaled. A tall wooden ladder was halfway down the expanse of shelving.

She jumped as a loud thump sounded, followed by a gasp from Emma and the sound of a lumbering mechanical beast roaring to life. Molly sighed. "The AC."

"I saw an air conditioner and a dehumidifier back there beyond the stairs," Emma whispered. She looked down at the bottom of the shelves. "Look. Someone has tried to make this basement as safe for books as possible. The shelves begin at about a foot up."

Molly looked. The bottom foot of the shelves looked like solid metal.

Emma bent over and ran her hand along the bottom of the bookshelf. "But there's a little rust along the bottom edge." She stood up. "Who would risk storing books in a Southern basement, with all the danger of flooding?"

Molly said, "Someone must have really wanted to keep them hidden." She scanned the shelf with her flashlight, but it was hard to see any titles. Many of the volumes looked like leather, vellum, or parchment—many were old rag paper. Some spines showed faded gilt lettering and designs. Some looked in good condition, others had frayed, faded covers. And some had no covers at all. She ached to touch them, to rub the soft sheepskin, smell the cowhide, stroke the gilt letters on the frayed spines, sniff the foxed, stained paper.

As her eyes followed the small circle of light, she could feel Emma's breath on her neck. Sensation trickled across her shoulders and down her arms. She could almost feel the outline of Emma's body behind her, like a tangible shadow. Molly caught a whiff of the other woman's light scent, floral, maybe jasmine, warmed with a tinge of sweat.

The frustration of closeness to books and the woman behind her was too much. "Oh, it's impossible," she burst out, louder than she had intended.

"Shhh!" whispered Emma.

"I can't see what anything is without touching them."

Emma said as though thinking aloud, "Well, the police are probably not interested in these books, since they haven't taped them off or taken them away or anything." She nodded. "Here, I'll hold the flashlight."

Molly shot her a quick grin. Then, hands released, Molly reached up, running her fingers along the spines on the highest shelf she could reach, her mind now absorbed only by the books.

"What about fingerprints?" Emma whispered. "Here." She proffered a cotton handkerchief.

"Thanks." Molly whispered, taking it.

That warning note had looked centuries old, so Molly looked for the oldest books. Her fingers found an ivory vellum volume, its edges curled toward the middle. "My professor at the Bodleian Library said, 'A vellum book never forgets it was a sheep.'"

"You went to Oxford?"

"Special class for book collectors at the Bodleian Library a few years ago," murmured Molly. "Look, these pages must have come from its side." Her fingers caressed the smooth cover as she gently pulled it from the shelf. Raising the book close to her eyes, Molly read in a reverent voice, "Nicolas Flamel, *Hieroglyphical Key, Being an Explication of Alchemical Figures which He Caused to be Painted upon an Arch in St Innocents Church Yard in Paris.*" She gingerly opened the cover. All the pages were loose and many looked like some insects had been nibbling. "Oh, my god, 1624," she whispered. "Too bad it's in such bad condition."

She started to turn a page, but it was page 32, none of the pages were in order. "Note probably isn't by Flamel—his first initial is 'N,'" she said. She definitely didn't want to harm the book. How was she going to find which one that note came from? She held the Flamel a moment longer, pressing it against her chest and giving it a little pat. Then she wiped it with the handkerchief and slid it gently back onto the shelf.

Looking further along the shelf, Molly covered her hand with the handkerchief and pulled out a volume in morocco leather with the title, *The Discoverie of Witchcraft,* in gilt on the spine. The edges of the pages were also gilt but mostly untrimmed, as she found when she slipped a finger in and encountered uncut pages. It was copy 334 of a limited edition of 1,275, printed in 1930 with an introduction by Montague Summers.

Emma leaned over and lightly touched the book. "Reginald Scot," she said in a soft voice. "That book was burned by James the First."

Molly looked at her. "I thought you weren't into occult."

"My Ph.D. is in early modern literature. Renaissance, it used to be called. Scot was trying to disprove much of what was said about witchcraft, but King James was a great believer in it, so he thought the book was dangerous."

"Obviously all copies weren't burned," Molly said.

"That's a myth about James burning all the copies. Lots of them survived. People kept and hid their copies of forbidden books until it was safe. Elizabethans and Jacobeans were used to changes in what was legal and what wasn't. They hid their missals; they hid their Tyndale Bibles. Shakespeare's dad hid his will in the attic."

"Why would he do that?"

"It was in a Catholic format."

Molly raised her eyebrows. Emma kept surprising her.

Emma said quietly, "We need to hurry. It's getting late."

"Just a little longer," murmured Molly. "We've hardly looked at any of the books."

"I wish we did have time to discover what all might be here." Emma gazed up and around at the bookshelves.

A volume that looked like it was put in backwards caught Molly's eye, but she remembered that in the fifteenth and sixteenth centuries, some were shelved that way. A chain attached to the spine would hold it to a shelf with the fore edges exposed She slowly pulled it out.

"What is it?" Emma shone the flashlight on it.

Molly carefully opened the delicate book. It had no cover, only a title page. "This looks like Latin. Damn! I wish we had better light." She smelled the musty scent of the thin paper. She pulled the book away from her face and peered at the title page. As she focused her eyes, she read a few words of the Latin. "Henrici," she read. "Henrici Cor. Agrippae—Cornelius Agrippa?"

She heard Emma close behind her. "Let me see." Emma took the book out of her hand and peered at it. "Cornelius Agrippa. *De Occulta Philosophia libri III.* This is one of the foundational texts of Renaissance ceremonial magic."

"You know about ceremonial magic?"

"I learned about it while researching Renaissance magic," Emma said absently. "This edition was published in 1833. The note is obviously older than this book."

Molly reached for the book, and Emma reluctantly relinquished it. She said, "How are we going to figure out which one it came out of?"

"Good question." Molly gently replaced the Agrippa on its shelf.

Emma said, "This sounds like a possibility for one of your grimoires: *The Dragon Book of Essex*. Sounds innocent until you read the subtitle: *Grimorium Synomosia,* blah blah blah, *Being a Grammar of Quintessential Sorcery, Containing the Sacred Rites and Formulae Undertaken in the Mysteries of the Great Dragon.*"

Molly pulled the note out of her bag and compared

the paper. "This doesn't feel the same to me," she said, carefully opening it and fingering the thin, stained title page.

"Likely seventeenth century," Emma said. "Maybe we should take pictures of the books that seem to have magical rites so we can figure out which ones might contain a warning."

"Are you proposing we stay all night?" Molly felt a bit wicked.

"No! It won't take that long. I'll use my phone." Emma took her phone out of her pocket. "Hold up the book for me."

For each book, after Emma took a picture of the cover, Molly opened to the title page and copyright page, if it had one, and Emma photographed those also.

૯૭૯૭

"What time is it?" Molly straightened up and rubbed her lower back. "We've been at this for hours."

"It's nearly eleven," Emma said, yawning. "We started work around nine. So far, we've found exactly nine books with magical rites or instructions in them. Nine, and we've only gone through three shelves."

"But if it's only eleven, that's early."

"Early? I'm usually in bed this time of night!" Emma said. "Besides, I have to pee."

"Just one more! I get a burst of energy around eleven." Molly took down a clamshell box and worked a manuscript out of it. She read: "*Lemegeton vel Clavicula Salomonis Regis.* How's your Latin?"

"Well, '*Regis*' is king, so something King Solomon. I don't think '*lemegeton*' is real Latin. I've never seen it before. 'Clavicle' is, of course, the collarbone." She laughed. "I'm getting silly." Flexing her fingers, she said, "Clavi, clav, clev, oh! Key, like the French '*clé*.'"

"Oh my god! It's the *Lesser Key of Solomon*. Remember I told you about the grimoire I had once? It was called the *Goetia: The Lesser Key of Solomon*. But that was a reprint. Most of these manuscripts were burned by rabid Christians. Oh, wow." She ran her palm over the surface of the vellum. "But I doubt this is the book the note fell out of, since it's in a box."

Molly's flashlight dimmed and went out, plunging them into darkness, except for the bright rectangle of Emma's phone.

"That's it! Let's call it a night," Emma said.

"Just when it's getting exciting," Molly said. "Just kidding. I'm ready to go after this one."

After Emma took pictures of the *Goetia*, she turned on the phone's flashlight so Molly could locate the clamshell box and slip the *Lesser Key* into it.

Molly said, "Now let's remember where we stopped."

"Why? You're not thinking about coming back?"

"We only made a little progress."

"No way! Once is enough for me."

"I've gotta get back in here. You don't have to come." Molly ground her teeth in frustration.

Emma groaned. "Come on. My phone's battery is about to die."

Molly said, "Let's hope the demons are appeased that we're leaving." She raised her own phone aloft and ran the flashlight app's light along the dark wall of books. Nothing but spines, row on row, fading into shadows. "Now, where did we come in?"

"I thought you left the entrance ajar."

"I did." A chill crept across Molly's suddenly tight

shoulders. "Damn!"

Molly held the phone aloft and waved its weak beam back and forth and down to the floor. "Okay, let's hunt for the opening we came through. Do you recall exactly where the stairs were in relation to it?"

"I think they were at an angle. We came in through the moving shelves, and the stairs are there—" Emma pointed. "About halfway down the middle of the book wall."

"Let's focus." Molly stepped closer to the bookcases. "It must have swung closed when I pulled the first book off the shelf. I don't remember noticing when it wasn't open any more."

Suddenly they heard a sound. Both froze. Molly heard Emma's quick intake of breath. A step. Footsteps, close. Coming from the room behind the bookshelves.

A man's voice said, "Someone's been here."

Her first thought was that the police had found the secret passage and come to investigate. She looked at Emma, who shook her head slowly and started to inch away from the book wall.

A woman's voice said, "How recent?"

"Since the last gathering."

Emma pocketed the phone, grabbed Molly's hand, and pulled her in the direction of the stairs. Board panels on either side of the steps formed a rough closet where paint cans, brooms, and tools were stored. In the dark, they felt with their feet and hands until they found their way into the little closet where they huddled together.

Molly heard a low, grating sound as though a heavy object was being pushed across the concrete floor. The bookcase was opening. Light flickered, casting shadows on the basement wall. They drew further into the closet. Molly heard Emma breathing rapidly.

Footsteps, more than one person, murmuring voices. A beam of light moved around. Whoever came in must be searching the shelves. Molly realized she was holding her breath, and slowly let it out. Emma started breathing deeply and exhaled with a soft whoosh.

Molly heard the snap of the light cord being pulled. The male voice said, "Damn! The light's burned out." Molly thought, *We couldn't have turned it on anyway.*

The man said, "The Book is not here." He emphasized the word "Book" as though giving it an initial cap.

Molly thought, *The Book? They're looking for a particular book.*

"What do you mean, it's not here?"

"It's not on the shelf where it's supposed to be. Not anywhere near it either. They got it somehow."

The woman's voice said, "I told you we should have taken it and the other grimoires out earlier."

He said, "Bernard always said to leave them here. But let's not argue. The others will be here soon. It's nearly midnight."

"Grab the *Goetia*. It'll have what we need. Let's go back and get ready."

Molly wondered if he pulled down the same book that she and Emma had just touched, would he be able to tell? She shivered.

The sound of footsteps grew softer and faded out. Molly heard the heavy pushing sound again and a click. She could still hear muffled voices through the wall.

They waited and listened.

Molly whispered, "Something is missing. I wonder if the police took the books Buck was stealing?"

A woman's voice with a rhythmic sound, half singing, half chanting, was joined by others, as though in church.

"Let's go up the stairs, now," Emma whispered, "while they're busy. They won't hear us if we go quietly."

"Okay, let's go." Molly ventured out of the little closet, Emma close behind. Groping, they found the stairs and started up them, Molly first on all fours, Emma behind. The AC suddenly roared on, and Molly thankfully blessed it.

After about a minute of feeling their way up the steep steps, Molly encountered a solid wall. The door was closed.

She carefully felt for the handle and tried to turn it. "Shit," she muttered. It was locked.

"Here, let me try," whispered Emma. She stood on the top step next to Molly, pressing close to her, and worked the door handle.

"What are you doing?" whispered Molly.

"Debit card."

Molly heard the minute sounds of the card being slid in between the door and the frame, up and down, down and up. The door handle was being moved slightly back and forth. She could hear Emma's quick breathing, feel her hair pressing against her own face.

Just as Molly was about to decide this was hopeless, she heard a click as the tongue of the lock pushed back, and another click as the door handle turned and the door was pushed open.

They shoved themselves out into the upstairs hall. Molly whispered, "Wipe the door handle!" Emma pulled a handkerchief out of her pocket and wiped the door handles on both sides, then softly pushed the door closed behind them.

"Emma," Molly whispered. "You amaze me."

Emma's voice in the dark held a small note of triumph. "I locked myself out one time when I went to the garden and automatically turned the lock behind me. I had my debit card in my back pocket and figured out how to let myself in. Kind of scary how easy it is to break in without the deadbolt in place."

They tiptoed through the hall door to the living room and wove their way around the piles of books and other items stacked by the dealers over to the picture window. Molly peered through the narrow crack in the drapes. Thank goodness Dr. Booth hadn't taken them down yet.

She saw that the front door light was off, but a street light cast its circle across the lawn. The full moon was higher, not letting out much light beyond its own aura. Several cars were parked along the curb.

"Let's hope no one is in those cars," Molly murmured. "Or that nobody drives up late."

"They might have someone posted to watch," Emma muttered.

They stood a moment, looking out the crack in the drapes. Molly went to the front door and tried it. *Please, don't let the deadbolt be keyed*, she prayed.

It wasn't. Both locks were the kind that turned. *Luck is with us*, she thought.

Nobody had come in through this door tonight, Molly guessed. And Dr. Booth had been the last to leave through it. Once more, she covered her hand with the handkerchief to turn both locks to let them out.

Pushing open the door, she looked out to make sure no one was around. Nothing hindered them as they stepped out onto the stoop, closed the door behind them, and walked quickly, carefully not running, past the cars, around the corner to the van a block away. They didn't dare go through the backyard for fear of running into anyone going to or from the tunnel.

In the van, doors locked, key turned, and motor started, they did not speak until Molly had driven down the street and turned the corner.

Emma looked back. "No one's following us. If anyone saw us, they must have thought we were part of the group."

Molly's mind whirred. "Who were those people? Why were they in the room?"

"Full moon ceremony?"

Molly glanced at Emma. She knew about full moon ceremonies. What else did she know?

"They're certainly not Wiccans," Emma said. "Wiccans would be out under the full moon."

"Right. So these guys are something else. Could be…" Molly spoke slowly because she didn't want to put into words what she was thinking. "I read somewhere that where someone dies, the spirit is especially powerful and attractive to black magic practitioners."

"I thought that evil spirits were evil on earth too. Not that they can be made evil by a group of what—black magicians?"

"I don't know. But our man wasn't exactly ethical when he was alive, to say the least." For some reason, she was reluctant to speak Buck's name. After a moment, she added, "Maybe the book they were looking for told how to make a spirit do their bidding."

"Do you think it might have been the one that note fell out of?"

Molly drew a deep breath. "No way of knowing. But it might be."

"Then, if it is, it must have been one of the books he tried to steal."

"In that case, the cops may have it."

"That's good then, right? It's where it can't do any harm—if it could."

"Good? It's where I can't get at it!" Molly burst out.

"Oh, Molly. Do you really want to, now that we know what it was being used for?"

"Of course I do." Despite how the Goetia she had earlier made her feel, this time it was a treasure hunt.

CHAPTER 7
The Die is Cast

L. W. de Laurence (ed.), The Lesser Key of Solomon, Goetia: The Book of Evil Spirits, *1911, black cloth with gilt lettering and illustration of demon on front cover. Contains 200 diagrams and seals for invocation and convocation of spirits. Necromancy, witchcraft and black art. Reprint of a 17th century grimoire.*

On their drive back that night, Emma watched Molly as she drove, wincing as she put on the brakes a moment later than she herself would have. After the short conversation leaving the Booth house, neither talked much. They stayed with their own thoughts.

Emma had to admit that driving through the streets late at night was oddly exciting. She marveled at the quietness, the few cars on the streets, a sense of driving through a different city than the one she knew by day. Two persons stood on a corner, obviously arguing. Another walked quickly by, paying them no attention. A woman stood at a bus stop, looking weary, laden down with tote bags and purse kept close to her body. Emma thought how narrow and safe her own life had become.

As they turned off Juniper onto Tenth Street, passing

the site of the gay bookstore that had closed a few years ago, Molly said, "So are you going to the ABOG meeting this Sunday?"

"Not sure," Emma said. "I don't know many of the booksellers." Emma had just joined the Antiquarian Booksellers of Georgia.

"You can ride with me," Molly said. She gave Emma a quick glance, then back to the road.

"That would be nice," Emma said. She looked away out the side window, but still felt Molly's eyes. What color were they? "I hate to go places alone where I don't know anybody. Well, not many people, anyway."

"They're friendly when you get to know them. It's mostly men. There are a few other women booksellers in ABOG, but they don't live close enough to come to the meetings. Carol and Dan live in the mountains, and Cathy's in Savannah. We should go, though, because everyone will be talking about Buck's murder. The murderer might even be there! We can listen for clues."

"Clues?" Emma sat upright. "I didn't know we were trying to solve Buck's murder." She shot Molly a sideways glance. "I thought we were trying to find out what ancient tome that note fell out of."

Molly said in a soft voice, not looking away from the street. "I think they're related."

Emma drew in her breath. "This is all getting a little too complicated for me. Not to mention dangerous."

Molly nodded as they turned off Memorial onto the little side street where Emma's car sat in front of Oxygen. Pulling up beside it, she stopped the van.

"Well, thanks for the exciting evening," Emma said, unbuckling her seat belt and gathering her bag from the floor of the van.

"Emma, wait." Molly's voice was quiet. "Let's talk

a minute about this."

Emma tensed. "What is 'this'?"

"I know it's dangerous. If Buck's murder and that note and all this occult stuff in the Booth house are connected, we may find some really nasty people. Like I said, I'm not into the occult—well, except astrology and tarot. I know some Wiccans, and they're harmless, earth-loving, peaceful people. But I know there are some out there who practice magic that are not Wiccan. Some do necromancy or worship dark powers. And Doctor Booth's grandfather may have been one of those. If that's the case—" Molly seemed to be groping for words. "So—if you don't want to go on investigating this, I'll understand."

"If I don't, will you go on investigating it alone?" asked Emma.

Molly nodded. "I *have* to find that book." She pressed her lips tightly together.

Emma looked at the woman behind the wheel. Molly had seemed the opposite of an obsessed, fanatical person who would foolishly pursue something that might lead her into danger. But now . . . "I don't get involved in weird stuff," she said. "Or with weird people. And it makes me nervous to be around a murderer."

Molly looked down. She seemed disappointed.

Emma hesitated. "But I'm in."

Molly gave her a wide, crinkling smile. "I'm glad."

"Yeah, I'm glad, too." Emma kept looking into Molly's eyes. By the arc lights in the parking lot, she could now see they were blue. With thick, soft, pale lashes. *When did I get in so deep? What is it about Molly that makes me want to go along with this insane, dangerous plan?* For she was now committed. Committed to finding out who murdered Buck and to finding the book that had held that note. Committed to anything that would keep her with Molly.

CHAPTER 8
The Booksellers' Meeting

Alice Bailey, A Treatise on White Magic or The Way of the Disciple, *1934, blue cloth with gilt on spine and front cover. Astral energy, breath, eyes, hands, sounds, and thought forms.*

On Sunday afternoon, Molly arrived at Emma's bungalow, less than a mile from her own house. She usually didn't take care with how she dressed for an ABOG meeting, but today she had tried on three shirts before deciding to wear a blue ikat patterned camp shirt. It went with her eyes, she decided.

Emma's yard was full of robust flowering plants: several types of roses, oak leaf hydrangeas, cone flowers, zinnias, rudbeckia, and swamp hibiscus. Emma sat on her narrow porch in a patch of sunlight. An opened book lay on her lap, but she was looking out into the yard. When she saw Molly's van, she slipped the book into a large purse and hurried down the walk, her long, magenta tunic swinging over black tights. She pulled open the door of the van and jumped in, all flourish and color. Molly's eyes followed Emma's hand as the other woman pushed a strand of silver-streaked dark hair off her face. A single turquoise ring adorned the hand.

"Hi," Molly said. "I like that top."

"Thanks."

"Hope I'm not late."

"Just enjoying the sun. I brought out a book to read, but when I'm on the porch, I keep seeing things I need to do in the yard."

As the van pulled out of Emma's driveway, she buckled her seat belt. "So this meeting is in Marietta? Is it always there?"

"Lately it is. Fred and Sarah usually host. You probably met them at the Florida Fair."

"Fred led the meeting? Glasses, gray hair, beard?"

"Right. He and Sarah are old hippies who used to sell books and collectibles on the antique circuit. He started selling books exclusively about ten years ago. Focuses on science fiction and fantasy."

"Molly," Emma said haltingly, "let's not let anyone know we're looking into the murder, okay?"

When Molly saw that Emma was rubbing her knuckles, she answered, "Okay."

They drove to the end of a cul-de-sac where a scattering of trucks and vans were parked in front of a 1940's box of a house that had been added onto over the decades. A crowd of wildflowers and herbs populated the front yard. Molly liked it, though it was a bit more overgrown than even she preferred.

Sarah met them at the door, wearing a flowing, long skirt and peasant blouse, her gray hair waving about her shoulders. "Hi, Molly." To Emma, she said, "Didn't I meet you in Florida?"

"That's right," Emma said, extending her hand. "Emma Clarke."

"Come on in and get something to eat." Sarah gestured to the dining room, where booksellers were milling about, filling their plates with Mexican food. A teenager sat on a stool at the kitchen island, dipping chips into guacamole. Her phone lay on the counter next to her, and she stared at it while she guided the chips to her mouth.

"This is my niece, Kelly," Sarah said.

"Cousin," Kelly said, mouth turning down.

"Yes, but you call me 'Aunt Sarah.'"

"That's 'cause Dad won't let me call you just Sarah, and 'Cousin Sarah' sounds all Jane Austen." She turned her attention back to her phone and food.

"Yum," said Molly. "Enchiladas verde."

"And mango salsa," murmured Emma.

Molly glanced around at the familiar faces. She had known these people for over a decade. Now, she looked at them with new eyes. One of them might be a murderer. She stopped a second, a serving spoon laden with an enchilada halfway to her plate. Everyone here was bound to know by now that Emma found the body, that the two of them were the first to see it. Some of them might be suspecting her or Emma.

Beer, wine, and soft drinks were on the counter, and Molly grabbed a ginger ale. Balancing her plate in one hand and her drink in the other, she went into the living room, and sat next to Emma, who was already seated with her plate and plastic glass of white wine.

Across from Molly on the couch sat Elliott Warren. Molly had first met him when he owned a bookstore in the Virginia Highland neighborhood. Ever dapper, in pressed chinos and a neat, starched white shirt, his sweep of thick hair, silver as the rims of his glasses, fell over half his forehead. Elliott was originally from London.

Molly greeted him and introduced Emma.

"So nice to meet you, Emma!" Elliott always managed to make anything he said sound arch and snide. But his eyes appeared pleased, even a touch flirtatious. Once, in a parking lot, Molly had come upon him looking at his reflection in a car window. He had tilted his head and smoothed down one side of his moustache and smiled at himself. Molly watched him anew: was there a cold, sinister expression in his eyes that she had never noticed before? Could he be more than a self-involved dandy?

Fred raised his voice. "Everyone, we're about to get the meeting started. Let's get our food and gather here in the living room."

Harry sat down next to Molly. "Can you believe that estate sale? More excitement than usual, huh?"

Molly nodded and sipped ginger ale, gone almost flat, not like the first taste, all tingly and tickling her nose. She had always thought of Harry as a buddy, the bookseller closest to her in age and outlook, and somewhat hippy-esque. Harry was no stranger to weed. She'd run across him hastily putting something away in his messenger bag, behind the Coliseum in Florida, at a book fair two years ago. As she approached, a light fragrance of cannabis had floated unmistakably in the air. Could he be more than he seemed? That honest, easygoing manner, those casual hugs—could they conceal a secret life, even a capacity for violence?

Harry went on in a hushed voice, "What about Buck? Hard to believe. We saw him in line, and then—he's dead."

Elliott's clipped British voice rang high in the sudden silence. "He finally got what was coming to him."

A gasp sounded, along with several subdued clicks of tongues.

"Elliott," Harry said in a low voice.

"Come on," Elliott continued, "Aren't we all thinking that? After all, he's stolen from all of us at one time or another, am I right?"

Everyone glanced around the room or looked absorbed in their plates. Jay snorted. "Good thing there's no cops here."

"I've had enough with cops," Harry said. "I had two more sales I was going to on Friday, and I had to stay and answer questions."

"We all did," Jay said, chewing his enchilada.

Molly said, "Was everybody here at that sale?"

"I wasn't," Elliott said. "I don't go to estate sales."

Fred and a couple other dealers also said they hadn't been there.

Harry said, "There were some non-ABOG book people there too, like Michael. You know him, that engineer?"

Jay laughed. "Guy with a real job. That guy from Ohio, too, who sets up at Scott."

"Emma, you're the one who found Buck. Tell us about it," said Elliott, leaning forward.

Emma hesitated and looked down, seeming suddenly vulnerable in her tights and little black shoes. "It was a shock. I still haven't decided how I feel about it."

Molly, feeling unexpectedly protective, started to say something to draw away their attention from Emma. But Fred cleared his throat. "We're all saddened, I'm sure, by Buck's passing, but we came here for a meeting. So let's get started. We need to talk about the book fair."

Sarah passed around the agenda and sat down by her husband. Fred called the meeting to order. They began talking about the upcoming book fair, and Molly found herself on the book fair committee.

At the end of the meeting, Fred said, "If anyone would like to, you can join me in the back room to look at my books." He stood, leading the way to the add-on area he had built onto his house for the sole purpose of storing his stock.

Emma stood, murmuring to Molly, "I was wondering where the books were."

"Do you want to go look at them?" Molly asked. "I think I'll stay here." She hadn't finished her second enchilada. Besides, she wanted to listen to the booksellers for any information.

Emma rose to follow Sarah. "Do you all sell any children's books?" she asked.

Sarah laughed. "Oh, the books are all his. He loves the books, and I love the bookman." They disappeared through the passageway to the add-on, trailed by Jay.

Molly remained seated next to Harry, who settled back with his second beer.

Elliott crossed his legs and sipped his Guinness. "Once Buck stole a first edition of *Wise Blood* from Greg Anderson at *All About Books* and carried it over to Tom's. But Greg sent all of us with bookstores an email saying it had been stolen and that it had a clipped dust jacket. So when Tom saw it, he instantly knew where it was from."

Molly remembered that she had not seen either Greg or Tom, both bookstore owners and ABOG members, at the estate sale. That might rule them out.

Harry said, "When I had that warehouse on West Ponce, I'd occasionally have sales—certain books half price, seventy percent off, that kind of thing. I'd find Buck behind the counter or in the back where I kept the books I hadn't priced yet. Sometimes later I'd have trouble finding a book and I'd wonder—"

"I wouldn't wonder," Elliott interrupted. "I'd *know* it was Buck. Back when I was working with Linda at *Beat-up Books*, she caught him red-handed stealing a first Faulkner. She told him, 'Buck, I can call the police, or I can ban you from the store, it's your choice.' So he agreed not to come back."

"She should've called the cops," Molly said. "Once when I was in *Book Traders*, I saw him with a rectangular bulge in the back of his pants, so I went to the front counter and told them he might have stolen a book. You know what the clerk said? 'He's one of our best customers!'"

Harry snorted. "As long as you buy lots of cheap books, go ahead and steal a first folio!"

Elliott said, "He wouldn't know a first folio if it hit him in the head." He covered his mouth. "Oops!"

Molly looked from one to the other as she sipped her ginger ale. How did he know Buck was hit in the head? Could she rule him out as a suspect? Or had he been hiding in the basement?

"Were you there that time he and Michael got into it? They were about to start punching each other at the AAUW sale," Elliott said.

"No," Harry said. "I won't say anything, though, since you're not supposed to talk ill of the dead."

"You mean about who you wanted to see win a fight?" Elliott asked. "See, Buck told one of the volunteers that there was room for the books from a box on the floor, and that he'd help her put them on the table. So she'd hand five or so books to Buck who would put them on his side of the table. I saw a copy of Jimmy Carter's first book go from her hand, and then it disappeared. Michael and I were watching, and that's

Michael's kind of book, and he said, 'Buck, let the lady put the books on the table.' And Buck said, 'Mind your own damn business.' Michael yelled back, and it got worse from there."

Molly continued listening to the familiar stories about Buck's stealing books. Each bookseller had a story, yet no one had ever called the police. Maybe if someone had, Buck wouldn't have kept on stealing. And he might still be alive.

CHAPTER 9
Not Narnia

H. P. Blavatsky, The Secret Doctrine: the Synthesis of Science, Religion, and Philosophy, *1913, four volumes, third and revised edition, blue cloth with gilt lettering and design to covers and spine. By one of the major figures in Theosophy, this set outlines the tenets of the Secret Doctrine of the Archaic Ages, including the origin and evolution of the cosmos, karma, life after death, and the purpose of existence.*

Emma entered a long room, cool and dry, with rows of bookshelves resembling the stacks in a library. She rubbed her arms through her silky long sleeves as she walked slowly along the aisles between the shelves, looking carefully at each row, running her hand lightly along the spines. She didn't see any children's, YA, or illustrated classics. Lots of alternate worlds, all neatly jacketed in Mylar. A few oversized photography books. She heard Jay's and Fred's voices chatting a few rows over, Jay's rapid sentences about one bookseller after another, with Fred's deeper voice asking questions.

Intuition led her towards gold or silver leaf on spines or toward matched sets. She saw a set of green spines at the end of a row and hastened toward them. Aha! She was right: *Narnia.*

She pulled out the first book and opened it. *The Lion, the Witch, and the Wardrobe* had the price of the total set on the flyleaf. She stroked the spine. It was a lovely set in good condition, but unfortunately she couldn't make a profit on it, considering what illustrated sets like this were going for now. Maybe Fred had some individual first editions from the series.

Stooping down to a lower shelf, she saw a slim black volume and, on impulse, pulled it out. She ran her fingers over the pebbled cover and spine. Raised embossing on black morocco, no gilt, no contrast to the unrelieved black. Out of curiosity, she opened it to the title page. *"Against the Diabolical,* by C.S. Lewis," she read. A limited edition of 26 lettered copies with the letter "K" written in ink. Strange: a Lewis title she had never heard of. The title page was lightly freckled with foxing around the edging, with a small tear in the upper corner. The press was unfamiliar to her: Undercroft. She carefully turned the thin pages. She had started to read the introduction when a voice made her jump.

"Hey, Emma!" Jay called from the next row. "You might want to take a look at these Oz books over here."

"I certainly would. Thanks!" She felt annoyed; she had wanted to look more carefully at the Lewis book. She slipped it into her large leather bag. She would bring it back as soon as she had looked at the Oz books. She noticed the gap on the shelf where the book had been. Without knowing exactly why, she nudged the other books together so that the gap disappeared. Then she located Jay.

"Did you find anything good at that estate sale?" she asked.

"A few. You?"

"Some nice illustrated classics."

He ran a thin hand through his unruly hair. "Any photography?"

"No, but I found a Maxfield Parrish and some other coffee table books. I hated that we had to leave everything there."

"It's ridiculous. What difference would it make?" He stepped closer and lowered his voice. "It must have been awful to find him like that." His voice invited confidences.

Emma looked closely at him. She didn't know Jay that well. At the estate sale, he had been everywhere, dashing about, snatching up piles of books. Could he have found Buck taking a book he had his eye on and, his competitiveness taking over, bashed the hapless thief over the head? But she had seen Jay upstairs in the hall just as she heard the voices and the thud. So that scenario was out. She sighed and decided to give him a nugget of information. "It was horrible. I was going by the door, and I heard voices, then a noise like something heavy falling."

"Wow," said Jay. "You may have actually heard the murder being committed."

They were silent. Emma asked, "Was he really a book dealer or just a collector?"

Jay shrugged. "He said he was a collector. But then why was he so aggressive? It's us dealers who are supposed to be cutthroat." His face reddened as he added, "Not *literally* cutthroat."

"Molly warned me about him," Emma said. "He did try to push ahead of me in line."

Fred popped around the corner of a stack. "I think he was klepto. That's the only way to describe him. He didn't need to steal. He drove a Mercedes, so he must have had money. He probably could buy any book he wanted."

Emma remembered that Fred had not been at the sale, and she wondered whether someone not there might have had a better chance to kill Buck than someone who was. They would have to know about the tunnel. And the secret room. She had a chilling thought and looked at the booksellers with new eyes. Could Fred be into black magic? She had an image of that unruly grey hair topping a black magus's robe, or maybe nothing. She tried to suppress a giggle at the thought, but it came out as a sort of choking gurgle. Fred looked a tad alarmed.

"Here's the Oz books," said Jay, gesturing as though they belonged to him.

There were lots of them in different editions. As she started combing through them, she heard Fred say to Jay, "Who do *you* think did it?"

Jay said, "Anybody. He could'a opened a door to a room that was off limits, and somebody got mad that he was always going where he wasn't supposed to and pushed him down the stairs."

"Is that how he died? The news didn't say, just that the police suspect his death was not an accident."

So neither Jay nor Fred know how Buck was killed, Emma thought. *Or at least they're acting innocent.*

The two men started back to the main part of the house, and Emma decided to see if Molly was ready to leave.

After goodbyes, Emma climbed into the van, which was a little high for her, while long-legged Molly stepped in with ease.

When they were heading back into Atlanta, Molly

asked, "So, did you find out anything?"

Emma nodded. "I found out that Jay and Fred didn't know Buck had been hit on the head. Jay speculated that someone pushed him down the stairs."

"So the police haven't let that out," said Molly. "No wonder they asked us not to tell anyone that he had been struck. If Jay and them are telling the truth. Except Elliott made a remark about Buck being hit in the head. But you never know when to take Elliott seriously."

"Right. If I were the murderer, I'd act dumb, too."

As Molly sped up, turning onto the interstate, Emma's bag turned over on her big toe. She lifted it, and the thin black book fell out.

"Molly," she said, snatching it up. "I can't believe I did this, but I have one of Fred's books in my bag." She held it up.

"Huh?" Molly said.

"I was leafing through one of the C.S. Lewis books and Jay interrupted me, and I stuffed it into my purse. I planned to look at it later, and I forgot."

"Emma, you're not in the habit of stealing books, are you?" Molly half laughed.

"No! I am not a—a book thief! Well, I did take a hymnal from an Episcopal church once, but it was just to look up a song. I took it back the next Sunday."

When Molly didn't say anything, Emma went on, "I wanted to see if 'Morning Has Broken' was really a hymn. It is."

Molly blew out her breath. "So what did you take from Fred?"

"One by C. S. Lewis that I had never heard of before. I used to be into him, not just his children's books, but his essays also. I meant to put it back, but I forgot. I'll mail it back tomorrow," Emma said.

The van turned off I-20 and rattled along Boulevard, surrounded by Victorian houses, leafy yards, and small businesses. They passed a favorite place of Emma's, Victoria's Market and Deli. A couple sat outside on the bench eating sandwiches. She didn't want to end her time with Molly, so she said, "Hey, let's stop and have a bite to eat."

"Didn't you get much to eat at Fred's?"

"That was brunch. Now it's suppertime." She hesitated. "And...I want to talk some more."

Seated at a table in Victoria's, eating their sandwiches (Reuben on rye for Molly, American Veggie on whole grain for Emma) and drinking bottled lemonade, they discussed what had happened.

"Why did you put the book in your bag in the first place?" Molly asked.

"I don't know. I did it automatically."

"Maybe Screwtape made you do it."

Emma laughed. "Or maybe it was the spirit of Buck."

"Ha! That's more like it."

Emma wiped her fingers and reached into her bag. "Here, let me show it to you."

They pored over the little volume, careful to keep it away from their sandwiches. "It sounds like one of Lewis's radio talks," Molly said. "It has that affable, cheerful, slightly ironic British tone. I think Americans like him so much because of that."

"You, too!" Emma said. "I thought I was the only person who looked at Lewis in any kind of skeptical way. Almost everyone I meet venerates him. Oh, I don't mean he's not sincere, or that he's not a marvelous writer. And his knowledge of medieval and Renaissance literature—oh, my goodness. Have you read any of his literary criticism?"

"No," admitted Molly. "I was an English major, but I focused mainly on modern literature."

"Lewis could make the history of medieval romance seem exciting. I was so into courtly love for a while." Emma felt her face go warm. "The Platonic idea of courtly love, that is," she added. She seized a plastic fork and stabbed a large slice of Portobello mushroom that had fallen out of her sandwich.

"Anyway," Molly said, "this looks like a diatribe against what he calls 'the diabolical': anything from earth magic to astrology to dark magic and Satanists. He lumps them all together."

"Yes, I find that a bit annoying." Emma tasted the last of the tart lemonade and looked at her watch. "Since you drove out to May-retta, how about I buy you a beer? You do like beer, don't you?"

"Sure and sure."

"What kind do you like?"

"They sell Dragon's Milk Stout. Have you tried it?"

Emma said, "Not yet, but I can't think of a better beer to go along with C.S. Lewis."

Molly laughed. "You didn't happen to steal any Tolkiens whilst perusing our host's books, did you?"

Emma grinned and shook her head as she started toward the cooler case.

When she returned to their table, lugging a four-pack, Molly said, "You plan for us to drink all that? They are kind of strong."

Emma laughed. "That's the only way they sell it." She set the pack on the table. "I thought we could take them back to my house and talk more. That is, if you want."

"Sounds like a good idea," Molly said. "I can't stay

long, though. My dogs will want their evening walk before long."

"Dog people!" Emma said.

"Are you a cat person?"

Emma nodded. "I had a sweet cat, but she died about six months ago."

"I'm sorry," Molly said. "Do you miss her terribly?"

"Yes," Emma said. "She had this little voice like a squeak, and she didn't say much." She remembered how when she came home from a trip and Ellie would let out a short 'mwow' and run out the door. "But, you know, sometimes I think it's easier without a pet. Especially now that I'm traveling to book fairs. And I'm often away from the house all day. Cats generally don't mind, but I used to think I neglected her." She shook her head. "As bad as it sounds, I'm often glad to be pet-free."

"I do understand," Molly said. "Pet sitters aren't cheap."

"What kind of dogs do you have?"

"Russian Wolfhounds, Dmitri and Blavatsky. They're huge." Molly's voice became more lively. "Dmitri is larger, all muscle. Blavatsky is fluffier, but they both have thick hair."

"Blavatsky? Wasn't she that Russian occultist?"

"Madame Blavatsky was a Theosophist who wrote *The Secret Doctrine*. I've got two three-volume sets. One cheap and the other a pretty leather copy. It's really dense. About the cosmos and such. A blend of science and religious slash esoteric knowledge. I prefer her shorter treatises such as theosophy and reincarnation." Molly balled up her sandwich wrapper and tossed it into the garbage bin.

"And Dmitri?"

"I've long had a fascination with Russia. It's a name I like. Anyway, the dogs are full of energy and need two walks a day if I'm gonna get any peace. Last week I had to replace my front window because they go berserk when a dog walks by my house, or, as my brother likes to say, if someone is walking in the park two blocks away."

"They busted through the window?" Emma wasn't sure she wanted to meet these berserker dogs.

"They didn't go through the window, just hit against the glass and cracked it. I don't think they were trying to get out. They wanted to let the dogs walking by know that this is Batsky and Mitri's house." She let out a sharp laugh. "I bet when the glass broke, they ran and hid. Batsky is really nervous. She acts tough because she's scared, not because she's scary."

"Well, let's go so you can get home to your dogs before dark. Wouldn't want them to think you'd forgotten them."

Molly gave her a sharp look and said, "I am devoted to my dogs. Anyone who knows me knows that."

Emma nodded. "Understood." She gave Molly a half smile that Molly, after a moment, returned with a wide, warm grin that made Emma think that these dogs might not be so alarming after all.

CHAPTER 10
Dragon's Milk

Montague Summers, The History of Witchcraft and Demonology, *1926, blue cloth with gilt lettering on spine and gilt symbol on front, part of "History of Civilization" series. Historical view of witches throughout the centuries and countries.*

Molly and Emma were on their second beer each, sitting on Emma's front porch as the evening fell around them. Molly kept one eye on the sun's position and wished it would sink more slowly than usual. In summer she often walked Dmitri and Blavatsky around eight since it stayed light. She was reluctant to leave.

Emma leaned toward her. "Molly? Can I ask you something?"

"Yes?"

"When you picked up that note, did you, I mean, was it...?" She hesitated.

Molly put down her beer and looked at Emma. "What?"

"As if someone *wanted* you to pick it up?"

Molly gazed over Emma's shoulder at the red Knock-out roses with the Perillas growing among them.

Weeds, but Emma seemed to be cultivating them. "I don't know. I guess I was surprised to see something so old and so mysterious. And I wanted to figure out who SF was." She took another sip of the dark beer. She liked stouts and porters better than those hoppy beers that were all the rage at taverns. "I just slipped it in my bag so I could study it more."

"That's what I did. Don't you think it's odd that a book thief dies, then two upstanding dealers like us start stealing books?"

"Hey, I picked up a one-page note. I didn't steal a book."

"You know what I mean. We each took something without forethought. See?"

Molly looked at her. "You're right. That is odd." She found it hard to meet her new friend's eyes. As she usually did when something made her uncomfortable, she changed the subject. "Can I use your bathroom?" When she stood, she felt a little wobbly. This beer, this Dragon's Milk, *was* strong.

"Sure. I have to go, too."

As Emma led her down the wide hallway filled with books, Molly lurched a little, and Emma caught her elbow.

"Careful."

Molly said, "I think you've gotten me drunk." She grinned as she closed the bathroom door. It had been a long time since she'd had two beers, let alone two high-octane stouts. Before leaving the bathroom, she splashed water into her eyes and grinned at her reflection in the mirror to see what her tipsy face looked like to Emma.

While Emma took her turn in the bathroom, Molly scanned the shelves in the hallway. There was a lot of fiction, including science fiction and mysteries, most with female detectives. She also took a peek into Emma's bedroom with a neatly made-up bed and a red floral quilt. She turned back to the bookshelves and straightened up, innocent, at Emma's approach.

"Well, I better take off lest the hounds go crazy," Molly said.

"Are you okay to drive? You didn't tell me these stouts were so strong."

"I'll be all right. It's a short distance." Molly paused at the door. "I'm gonna look into some of my books and try to figure out who SF is."

They stood awkwardly in Emma's doorway. Molly started to hold out her hand, but instead opened her arms, and they had a quick hug goodbye. Molly liked the feel of Emma in her arms, and she held on a little longer than Emma did.

"Bye," said Emma softly. "Call me."

Molly felt a dance in her step as she walked to her van in the cooling evening air. And it wasn't the Dragon's Milk.

CHAPTER 11
Back to the Basement

Anonymous, Our Unseen Guest, *1920, brown boards with cloth spine and gilt lettering and embossing on front, black lettering on spine. A couple contacts spirits via a Ouija board.*

Molly couldn't get her mind off the books in the basement library. She finally called Dr. Booth and asked if he was interested in selling them.

He growled, "How do you know about those books?"

Molly, not expecting such an abrupt response, felt her mouth go dry for a moment. But she rallied. "I was one of the people who found Buck. I couldn't help noticing that they were occult-type books, and that's one of my bookselling specialties. I'd like to look at them if you are willing to sell."

Dr. Booth didn't speak for a moment. When he did, his voice still grated. "Those books are old, dirty, falling apart. I deliberately didn't put them out at the sale because they're not worth anything."

"I'd still like to take a look," Molly said, tilting her head towards her cell phone, shoulders bent, trying to hear his voice through Batsky's sudden, loud bark. Dmitri also began to bay, and both dogs rushed to the door, paws scuffling on the bare wood of the floor. The mail carrier had arrived. Molly sighed and drew on all her patience. "I sell esoteric and occult books, and I think I might find some that would interest my customers."

"Well, they're esoteric all right. Don't have a clue why Grandpa wanted books like that around. But if you think you could find anything to buy, then come on over."

Maybe he saw dollar signs. They agreed to meet at the Booth house on Thursday at seven in the evening.

Arriving on Friar Tuck Lane at dusk, Molly saw Dr. Booth's car in the driveway. No lights were on in the house or outside. The wide lawn was half in shadow, and she couldn't see the porch very well. Molly wished for a moment that Emma were with her. But this was a buying trip, and these were not Emma's type of books. She went to the front door and knocked.

She waited and knocked again. No sound, nothing. Had he forgotten they were going to meet? The front window was covered by drapes, but where it was pulled back at a corner, she saw groupings of objects the dealers had left last Friday. At least tomorrow she could get the books she had stacked up.

She peered at the piles, trying to read titles of the other dealers' finds. Suddenly, a young woman's face appeared, looking right at her. Molly jumped back, heart in her throat. The girl called, "Da—ad!"

She heard footsteps inside. Running back to the door, she was just in time to be greeted by Dr. Booth as he yanked it open.

"Ah, hi, Dr. Booth," she said, feeling as though she

had been caught in the act of something.

"Miss O'Donnell," he said brusquely.

She waited to be invited in, shifting from one foot to another.

Dr. Booth waved his hand impatiently. "Come on in if you're going to. I can't stay long." He glanced at his watch.

Molly got the hint. "So let's go look at the books."

As she followed Dr. Booth, he waved his hand at the young girl, saying, "This is my daughter Kelly."

Molly said, "Oh, hi. I didn't recognize you. We met at Sarah and Fred's."

Kelly muttered "Hi" without removing her earbuds or looking up from her phone.

No wonder she didn't hear me knock, thought Molly.

At the bottom of the stairs, Dr. Booth pulled the light cord, and this time the single bulb came on. Molly looked up and once more felt that overwhelming sense of awe wash over her in the presence of old books. The wall of volumes seemed to lean and swell towards her, pregnant with their contents as she gazed slowly around and up. Illuminated by the brilliant glare, she saw dusty leather covers, their gold leaf fading, interspersed with loose leaf bundles of what might be parchment or even vellum, bound together with ribbon so faded it had forgotten its original color. This time she noticed newer cloth covers with titles in block letters pressed in among the older volumes. The collection was even more impressive at a second viewing.

All these books surrounded her with their promises of other worlds, other times, other knowledge hidden from ordinary life. She had felt this awe and wonder when she first entered a library at the age of six, and even more so at college when, researching her senior thesis, she had timidly ventured into a high-ceilinged, gothic-arched room with card catalogs—ancient technology!—and a desk with helpful guardians who would bring out to you whatever you asked for. And when she went to the Bodleian in Oxford—well, it was like Harry entering Hogwarts for the first time.

Molly sneezed and returned to the present and the basement with an impatient dentist standing next to her, rocking on his heels.

"I actually found a catalog of these books in Granddad's desk," Dr. Booth said. "I can give you a copy. Would that help? Unless you want to buy the entire collection."

Molly did want the entire collection, lusted after it in her bones. But she knew that there were too many for her home office, and she would have to get a rental unit to store them. She said, "Yes, that would be very helpful." *Well,* she thought, *this is sure a turnabout from his attitude the other day. Maybe he's talked to one of the book dealers.*

Dr. Booth went upstairs, leaving her for a moment among the treasures. She lightly stroked a calfskin spine, half torn from its boards. Pressing the leather to the spine, as if to fuse them back together, she started to pull the book out when the dentist promptly reappeared with a stapled sheaf of papers.

"Look, I've really got to run," he said. "Why don't you take this home and look through it?"

"I'll bring it back tomorrow."

Dr. Booth shook his head. "I had several copies made."

What a shyster! she thought. *He did that after he talked with me and realized someone might pay good money for these books. He's going to give catalogs to other book dealers. Wonder who?*

Molly set her teeth in a flash of competitive anger. She would not be outbid by other dealers. "What are you asking for the whole collection?"

Dr. Booth gave her a narrow-eyed look. "I haven't decided yet. I thought I'd send catalogs to booksellers who list occult or esoteric as a specialty. Then take bids for the collection."

Damn. He did talk to other book dealers. She wouldn't have to bid against just other ABOG dealers, but Trailblazers in Ontario, Whisper Books in New York and other big time booksellers, people with space and staff to handle the volume of books. Maybe it would be worthwhile to find a space to store them. And while old Mr. Booth may have cataloged them, did he include criteria that she would need to include in her descriptions: condition, size, former owner's inscriptions or bookplates? She'd have to do all that before she could list them online. Molly felt suddenly as though the wall of books were about to tumble forward and fall on her.

"Have you sent the catalogs out yet?" She tried to sound casual.

"I just had the copies made today. I've been so busy getting ready for this estate sale from hell."

Molly thought fast. "Since I called you first, couldn't you give me the first crack at them? Then if I buy something, you can write "Sold" on the other catalog copies." She gave him what she considered her most charming smile, head tilted and a slight widening of eyes.

"Well, I don't know." Dr. Booth stepped back. "I want to get the best price for them."

Right. They were old and ragged and dirty a few

days ago. "I'll give you a good price for the ones I want. Besides, I'm local. I can pick them up. If you sell them out of state, think of what a hassle it would be to ship them."

Doctor Booth rubbed his temples. "All right. I'll hold off on mailing the catalogs for a week. In that time, you either make an offer for the ones you want or what you will pay for the whole collection."

Molly hastened up from the basement and out the door, almost running to her van.

CHAPTER 12
Emma Makes a Discovery

K. K. Doberer, The Goldmakers: 10,000 Years of Alchemy, *1948, green cloth with gilt on spine. Includes many magicians/alchemists throughout history, including Nicholas Flamel, Albertus Magnus, Edward Kelley, and Johann Goethe.*

On Monday, Emma had received an urgent editing job for a dissertation on Georgina Burne-Jones. She didn't finish until Thursday, and then she went to the library looking for books that might reveal who SF was. Now she had been hunched over her desk for three hours, a stack of books from the university library beside her. She had just finished peering through the index and chapter headings of a book on alchemy. Nothing. She picked up the photocopy of the paper that Molly had taken and stared at it. *SF*? She stood and stretched. Her eyes wandered over her shelves to the books she had used for her dissertation on Emilia Bassano Lanyer, an early feminist writer who had published a volume of poetry in 1611 calling for women's equality. She scanned the titles and stopped when she saw A.L. Rowse's book *Sex and Society in Shakespeare's Age: Simon Forman the Astrologer.*

Simon Forman? Emma looked back at the book's spine. She slowly took it off the shelf and stared at it. *SF*. She looked at her photocopy of the mysterious warning note that Molly had picked up. *What an idiot I've been*, she thought. *SF is Simon Forman!* She held the photocopy in her hand that had unaccountably started to shake. The original might have been handwritten by Simon Forman himself.

She looked for her cell phone and found it under a sun hat on the coffee table. Both of her hands were shaking as she punched in Molly's number.

"Damn!" she said as she heard Molly's recorded greeting. "Hi, Molly," she said. "I know who *SF* is! Give me a call as soon as possible."

CHAPTER 13
Sharing Discoveries

E. M. Butler, The Myth of the Magus, *1948, green cloth with gilt on spine, black dust jacket. Examination of magicians including Eastern magi, Moses, Virgil, Dr. Faust, John Dee, Madame Blavatsky, and Rasputin, concluding that their lives have similarities.*

Molly couldn't wait to tell Emma. Driving around the corner from the Booth house, she groped one-handed for her cell phone from the bottom of her tote bag, found it, pulled it up, and with one eye on the road called Emma, only to hear her recorded voice.

"Emma!" she said. "I've got news. Call me. Oh, this is Molly." She stared at her phone, willing it to ring, and noticed the symbol indicating that she had voice mail. She drove to the little park and pulled up under a street light to listen to the message. She laughed. They had called at the same time. She called Emma again.

"Hello! Molly?"

"Yes, it's me. Who's *SF*?"

Emma replied, "Simon Forman!"

"The astrologer? Lived the same time as John Dee?"

"Yes! What do you think?"

"Sounds plausible. Good work, Sherlock."

"So you said you had news, too."

"There's a catalog. Dr. Booth had it photocopied when he realized I was interested in the basement books, I'm sure. It will really help us to narrow down the list of books that the note could have come from. Did Simon Forman write any books?"

"He wrote a lot but published only one book in his lifetime, on latitude and longitude, of all things. He wrote a diary, autobiography, and casebooks with his clients' astrological charts. It's all in the Bodleian Library. A. L. Rowse was the first to edit and publish it with an introduction."

"So if Forman wrote that note," mused Molly, "it could have been in any of the books in Booth's collection written before or during Forman's lifetime. What are his dates?"

"Born mid-1500's. He correctly predicted the date of his own death in 1611. But—here's the connection with the Booth library—he was involved in necromancy, summoning spirits, and what sounds to me like black magic. He helped Frances Howard, Countess of Essex, by giving her a potion to make her husband impotent so she could divorce him and marry her lover. Little wax poppets, similar to voodoo dolls, were found in his house. They were shown in the courtroom as evidence."

"Wow," Molly said. "I'll take a look at the catalog soon as I get home tonight. I'd better go now. I still need to walk the dogs."

"All right. Talk to you later."

At a stoplight at the end of the Sherwood Forest subdivision, Molly picked up the catalog and turned on her car's overhead light. Each entry was numbered in order by subject. The first category was Alchemy, followed by Astrology. Her thoughts were interrupted by a honk. The light had turned green.

※ ※ ※

At home, Molly sat in her favorite chair with her feet propped on an old trunk she'd gotten from an estate sale out in the country. She'd walked the dogs and given them Nyla Bones so she'd have some peace and quiet. They were lying in front of her like two large, furry commas, curled around the bones. The peaceful sounds of crunching filled the room, along with the occasional thump of a tail and a canine groan of satisfaction. She flipped through the listings, looking at the categories.

Whoever made this list was no bibliographer. In each category, some of the books were listed by title, then author, some in reverse order. Maybe it was a file that was added to with new acquisitions. And there were no descriptions of condition. She wanted to read it all, but she needed to concentrate on finding what intrigued her most—which book the note fell out of. There were categories for Magic Spells, Magic (Black), and Magic (White). The *Goetia* she had seen on the shelf was in Magic (Black); other grimoires were in a subcategory under Magic Spells. Molly shook her head. Dealers would snort in disdain at the lack of organization and lack of important information, such as edition, printing, illustrations, or condition. They would think the seller was a rube. If they got past the disorganization and actually found what was in the collection, they would lowball their offers or write for more information. She allowed herself a small chuckle.

Batsky looked up expectantly and whuffed. Dmitri, ever the follower of his sister the Alpha, whuffed too and tried to climb on Molly's lap. "Good boy!" she said, scratching behind his ear. "Now go lay down!" He didn't move and was blocking her view of the catalog. Placing her hand flat against his chest, she pushed him off, not without difficulty. The dog threw himself down on the rug, his beautiful long nose between his paws, eyes cast down.

With a pencil, Molly circled grimoires that had dates earlier than 1611. At the end of the grimoire list were two anonymous manuscripts: *A Boke of Secret Knowlege by A Learned Doctor* and *Calendarium Naturale Magicum Perpetuum*. Neither had a date nor any indication of ever having been published, but were noted as circa 16th century, so she circled them. No way to tell what they looked like from this catalog. She would have to look at them again when she went back to the library. Her spirits lifted. "Goody!" she said aloud. Both dogs jumped to their feet. "Okay, who wants to go to bed?" she called. Dmitri headed to the dog door to relieve himself, and Blavatsky ran toward her crate. Molly followed, turning out the lights. In the dark she wondered, *What if spirits were all around, bound to earth, connected to places?*

CHAPTER 14
Emma Makes Another Discovery

Aleister Crowley, 777 Revised: A Reprint of 777 with much additional matter by the late Aleister Crowley, 1955, limited edition of 1100 copies. Quarter vellum and blue cloth with gilt lettering on vellum spine and front cover. A Qabalistic dictionary of ceremonial magic, oriental mysticism, comparative religion, and symbology. Also a handbook for ceremonial invocation.

Emma suddenly remembered that she had not mailed the C.S. Lewis book, *Against the Diabolical*, back to Fred. She got out her mailing supplies, took up the book, and turned it over. The back cover showed a picture of Lewis with a pipe, looking saturnine. Opening it, she glanced at the flyleaf. "This slim volume, one of Lewis's lesser-known works . . . incisive thought and erudition . . . clarifying Christian thought for the modern man." Still puzzling that she had never heard of this book, Emma turned the page and began reading the introduction.

Lewis, in his usual engaging style, told of an incident that had happened decades ago. He had been walking across a green at his college in Oxford, when he met a student of his who was excited over a book he had, a seventeenth-century manuscript book of spells. A small, slim sheaf of pages, loosely bound with faded ribbon, *A Boke of Secret Knowlege by A Learned Doctor*. It contained astrological and alchemical charts and symbols, as well as drawings representing the Sun, Mercury, the Moon, etc. Lewis was turning through it when he found a loose leaf, slightly smaller than the book's pages. He flipped the leaf over, revealing the picture of a demon's face underneath. He started to turn the page, but his student stopped him, placing his hand over the demon, saying that what followed was only for the initiated.

Lewis told his student to be careful about anything to do with demons or black magic. But the younger man invited him to come that evening to the banks of the Isis where he and some friends were holding a full moon circle. He said, "We practice magic, both dark and light." Lewis explained that there was no such thing as white magic, that all that was not of God was of the Devil. But his curiosity was aroused, and so he decided there would be no harm in attending just to see what was going on.

So that evening, Lewis went with his friend and met several other young men by the banks of the river Isis that flows through Oxford. As they watched, a full moon rose, turning the trees and shrubs lining the river into mysterious black shapes and flooding the meadow with light as bright as day. They formed a circle. One of the young men began to chant, and the others joined in. They seemed to know the words to the chant, which were not Latin or any other language Lewis knew. As they chanted, they grew more entranced and bespelled. Lewis was becoming uncomfortable and thought about leaving. Suddenly the chanting stopped, and a silence ensued. The young men all bowed deeply, and some fell to their knees.

Lewis backed away and hid in a clump of bushes.

What happened next, reader, I will not say. Yes, there were solemn words. There may have been nudity, unnatural acts, maniacal laughter, sobbing. The commonplaces of these pathetic cults are known to many nowadays. I confess I do not remember all. I only remember that a feeling of cold fear came over me, unexplained by what I saw or heard, and that a sense of danger and foreboding filled my heart. I slipped away and hastened back to my lodgings. My student missed our next weekly meeting. When I went to his room, his roommate curtly informed me that he had withdrawn. But he was dead by the end of the summer, and his family would not answer questions.

Emma blew out her breath and looked up. *Good Lord*, she thought. *Has Lewis turned into Stephen King? After all, he did write* The Space Trilogy, *and it got pretty diabolical. Is this for real?* She settled into her easy chair and pulled her feet up under her. She began to read and did not stop until she had finished the last page.

The main part of the book was not as compelling as the introduction, although Lewis's style carried her along. The points he made were his Christian beliefs, already stated: any venture into magic, sorcery, witchcraft, divination, fortunetelling, raising of spirits, Ouija boards, no matter how innocent in intent, opened up doorways into unseen worlds. Those doors were better kept closed, for once they were opened, dangerous forces could enter. (*Like inviting a vampire or a ghost into your house,* thought Emma.) The revivals of interest in magic at the turn of the twentieth century, from

Crowley to Waite, from Spiritualism to Theosophy, from tarot to devil worship, were all equally dangerous. And Earth magic, Paganism, Wicca, Cabala, astrology, even herbal lore, were examples of the modern world's falling away from the only path to grace that existed, that of Christianity. Most of these fads, as he called them, were childish and harmless, but they should still be avoided, lest harm slip through. The book ended with an afterword in which Lewis referred back to the incident that had prompted him to write.

I know not to this day where that manuscript is, nor do I care. I hope it has been consigned to the depths of the sea or thrown into a volcano. Perhaps it was destroyed during the bombing of London. That would be a fitting end for it. As for my student, I did learn more about his death and was sorry I did. I hope no more is said or written of that unfortunate youth, for if his fate were widely known, it would only bring more pain and shame to a family that has suffered enough. I pray for him still. In pax requiescat.

Emma looked up and around in a daze, almost bespelled herself. The house outside the circle of light from her reading lamp was pitch dark, and she felt so stiff that she groaned when she tried to stand upright. She had gone into the kind of book-induced trance that she loved, although when she came out of such trances, she often felt disoriented. The house looked unfamiliar, the walls oddly shaped, the table with its stacks of books as though she had not seen it before. She stood up and stretched. Thoughts of people, places, ideas not remembered for a long time strayed through her mind. *I'm eighteen. Or am I twelve? No, thirty-six. I'm in Chapel Hill. No, London; no, Atlanta. I am no one. No, I'm Emma Clarke. Who is that, Emma Clarke?* She shook herself and laid the book on the table, face down. On impulse, she set another book on top of it as making sure it stayed closed. She turned on several overhead lights. After checking the doors (they were locked) and turning on the porch light, she turned off the living room lights and headed to bed. She'd always been able to find her way in the dark. But this time, she turned on the hall light and left it on.

CHAPTER 15
Picking Up Books

Evelyn Underhill, Man and the Supernatural: A Study in Theism, *1928, red cover with gilt on spine, brown dust jacket. A theological look at where religion fits between the natural world and the supernatural.*

Molly knew Emma had arrived at her house when Blavatsky and Dmitri started barking at eight a.m. She'd only been up about fifteen minutes and felt a little groggy. When Molly and Emma decided to ride to the Booth house again to pick up their finds from the week before, Emma had volunteered to drive her old Volvo station wagon.

Dmitri ran to Molly's bedroom where she was tying her shoelaces. Blavatsky was still barking at the front door.

"What is it, guys? What's going on? Hey, it's Emma." After ruffling both dogs' fur, Molly said, "Dogs are gonna stay. I'll be back later. Be good dogs, okay?" They sat at either end of the sofa, looking resigned, as she opened the door.

"Morning," she called to Emma, who was starting to get out of her car.

"Good morning," her friend replied. "Sleep well?"

"Once I got to bed. Stayed up way too late looking at that catalog. What a mess. No order or consistency to it at all." Molly stretched the seat belt across her chest.

"I was up late myself," Emma said. "I meant to send the Lewis book back anonymously to Fred on Monday, but I got a rush editing job and forgot about it until last night. I started getting it ready and began to read the introduction. Then the first chapter, and then . . . well, you know how it goes."

Molly liked the satisfying click of a seatbelt into its holder. "I do. Not with Lewis, though. Not my cup of tea."

Emma started the car and headed toward Boulevard. "It was fascinating but disturbing. *Against the Diabolical* is a screed against everything occult, even herbal remedies and astrology. But the story he tells in the introduction is even more disturbing."

"What was disturbing about it?" Molly was having trouble paying attention to Emma's story so early in the morning. Her eyes felt scratchy. She closed them for a minute.

"In the introduction," she heard Emma's voice continue, "Lewis writes about an old manuscript." Emma's voice faded. Molly heard something about a circle of students by moonlight and C.S. Lewis hiding in the bushes. "Weird," she muttered. It had been almost four in the morning when she put down Mr. Booth's catalog of books. She would suggest they get coffee right after the sale, she decided. Her head felt heavy against the headrest, a bit loose on her shoulders. The typescript of the catalog wavered before her eyes. As she tried to read the type, suddenly she heard Emma's voice saying, "Wake up, sleepy head," and her eyes flew open.

"I wasn't asleep," Molly protested.

Emma took a sharp left onto Friar Tuck Road. "So you snore when you're awake?"

"Was I really snoring?"

Emma laughed. "Yes, you were putting on quite a symphony of sounds. Each one different from the one before."

Molly could feel her face grow warm with blushing. "I lived for nine years with my former partner, Julia, who swore that I snored, but if she said, 'quit snoring,' I would stop." She looked at Emma for any sign of a reaction. But Emma was looking ahead with a smile. *Well, one of us has finally said something*, thought Molly. She felt a little embarrassed that she had just spilled the beans, but at least now it was out in the open.

In front of the Booth house and in the driveway were several cars. A cluster of antique and book dealers stood in the driveway. As Molly and Emma approached the house, Molly saw Joyce standing on the stoop and heard her voice carrying clearly: "You may only buy what you have already chosen. The estate sale is ovah, so whatever you found last Friday, you may buy. We don't want anyone in any of the rooms other than the living room where your items are."

Jay said what Molly was thinking. "But what will happen to the books that we haven't had time to go through?"

"I had just started looking at the glass case when the sale ended," an antique dealer said.

A few people left the cluster and made their way back to their cars. "It's not fair not to let us shop today," Molly heard one say.

"What ya wanta bet they're being nosy and didn't come to buy anyway?" Molly said in a low voice to Emma. She added, chuckling, "We're nosy but we want to buy, that's the difference."

"I guess some people get a thrill entering a house where a murder took place," Emma said. "When I was growing up in the country in North Carolina, there was a farmhouse nearby where one brother killed another. It was abandoned, and kids were always breaking into the house and barn. Nobody knew where the murder took place. The kids were always daring each other to spend the night there. As far as I know, no one ever did."

Molly had noticed the slight southern accent. Now she knew—North Carolina.

"You grew up in the country?"

"Yep. Itty bitty little town. It wasn't even a town, just a post office address."

Molly filed away the information. She enjoyed getting to know Emma, little by little. Surprising that she had grown up in the country. Somehow she seemed urban to the core. Maybe it was her black tights and stylish shoes. Molly noted with approval the short black boots with buckles that Emma wore today.

As more people arrived, Joyce went through her speech again.

Jay asked, "When do we get in?"

"Ten o'clock. Same as last week," came Joyce's drawl.

Detectives DuBois and Richardson pulled up in a dark, nondescript car. DuBois waved to Molly and Emma. "Morning," she said, smiling, her blue eyes narrowing, her strong jaw jutting. "There's my partner Detective Richards." She indicated the tall African American man with her. "We'll probably want to interview you again."

"Now?" Emma asked.

Detective DuBois said, "No. We'll call you in."

Molly wondered what the detectives wanted to ask them about. Had they somehow found out about the night she and Emma broke in? Did they get their fingerprints? But fingerprints wouldn't meet a match unless hers were in the police database already, and she was sure they weren't. Not likely Emma's were either. When they were out of hearing of the detective, she turned to Emma. "I want to go back to the basement. There are a couple of manuscripts in the collection that I want to look at. They don't have dates or authors, so there's no telling how old they are. I'll call Dr. Booth again."

Once inside and reunited with her stash, Molly stood behind Jay. He had books overflowing in boxes and was paying for Harry's finds also.

Molly thought, *I bet Harry went to another estate sale this morning, probably the one with "Many, Many Books" in the title.* She would have gone there herself if she hadn't come here expecting to be able to shop some more.

As Molly started walking out of the house, Detective Richards approached. "Miss O'Donnell? Hold on."

"Detective Richards?" Her heart began to pound.

He nodded and said with a bland expression, "Anything you can remember seeing, hearing, feeling, or smelling can help us out."

"Smelling?" she said.

"Sure. Any strange odors, perfumes. Sometimes things come to people later." He reached into his pocket and handed her a business card. "Any time you remember anything you didn't mention to Detective DuBois, please call me."

"Okay. I sure will." Molly shifted her heavy bag full of books. The sun was well up and hot now, and she put on her sunglasses. Her heart slowed its pounding a little, but she was still almost panting with anxiety and also exhaustion from carrying her book bag up the long drive. She looked up to see Emma coming quickly along the walk, carrying her own book bag on its rolling cart.

"What did he ask you?" Emma said. She sounded a little breathless, and the crease between her dark brows cut deeper.

"Just to call if I remember anything."

"She told me again to expect a call." Emma talked faster. "They must suspect we've been down there and they've seen where we left tracks in the dust on the floor and where we took books off the shelf and put them back. If they take us in and fingerprint us, they may find our prints on the books! We might not have wiped all of them off."

They looked at one another in silence. Molly broke it with, "I need coffee. I was up 'til four last night." Molly didn't want to point out that Emma was told to expect a call but that Richards only told Molly to call them *if*. So Emma must be a suspect.

CHAPTER 16
Comparing Notes

Aleister Crowley, The Book of Thoth: A Short Essay on the Tarot of the Egyptians, *1944, Morocco leather, limited signed edition of 200 copies. Egyptian tarot invented by Crowley and designed by Frieda Harris.*

Emma had already had tea and a bagel that morning, so she only ordered a cup of Irish Breakfast. Molly indulged in a goat cheese quiche with asparagus, broccoli, and onions and a caramel latte.

Oxygen's tables were full of solo customers with laptops and phones, and students poring over their books. Outside, a whippet leaned his front paws on the window ledge so he could watch over his human. The only seats they could claim were at one end of a long table. At the other end sat two young men with shaved heads who leaned toward each other with private smiles.

Emma had been mildly fuming since before they arrived at the Booth house that morning. After debating with herself briefly, she decided to speak up. "Molly," she said, pulse starting to race, "You didn't sound very interested in the Lewis book. I was so excited that I almost called you last night, but I was afraid it was too late."

"I was probably still awake," Molly said. "Even after I got in bed, I kept reading that list. Why were you going to call me?"

"About the Lewis book," Emma repeated, feeling more frustrated. "I thought that manuscript his friend had was significant."

Molly took a bite of quiche and chewed, shaking her head. "Significant how? It didn't even have a name, did it?"

"As a matter of fact it does." Emma leaned forward. "*A Boke*—spelled b-o-k-e—*of Secret Knowlege.*"

Molly sat up straight, now alert, and said in unison with Emma, "*By a Learned Doctor!*"

The two men looked over at them, and then went back to staring into each other's eyes.

Emma's tea slopped over the edge of her mug. She set it down and swallowed. "How did you—?"

"It's in Dr. Booth's collection!" exclaimed Molly, a forkful of quiche forgotten halfway to her mouth. "It's one of several manuscripts that I circled, as a matter of fact. I remember it well—no date, the description says it's circa sixteenth or seventeenth century. Same as the warning note." She drew in her breath. "You don't remember whether Lewis said anything about a warning note?"

Emma shook her head. "What I have to do to get your attention! Just find a four-hundred-year-old manuscript with something occult about it?"

"Well, did he? Was there a warning in the manuscript?"

"Not exactly. He said that he was going to turn the page when—wait a minute! He said there was a loose leaf. Then his friend placed his hand over a picture of a demon and said that what came next was only for the initiated."

"Maybe that was the warning note!" Molly said. "But we won't know until we look at that manuscript. Compare the paper, the script." She absently ate the bite of quiche.

"Damn! I mailed the Lewis book to Fred this morning. I was so embarrassed about waiting so long, that I just wanted to get it out of the house." Emma took a sip. "I looked online this morning, but I couldn't find any copies that cost less than Fred's."

"I could ask on my listserv," Molly said, finishing the quiche and picking up pastry crumbs with her fingers, licking them.

Emma found herself smiling indulgently as she watched Molly lick her fingertips.

Molly noticed her looking and gave her a little grin, wiping her fingers with her tiny napkin.

Emma said, "This occult business doesn't sit well with me. Do you think that bad things have happened to people who possessed that book? Like that Oxford scholar?" She lowered her voice and looked around as though some evil being might be having a mocha at the next table. "I don't like to think such things are possible, but . . ." She let her voice trail off.

Molly took a final swallow of her latte. "Who knows? I don't want any part of black magic. I don't know how any good could come from it. That's why I won't sell books that tell you how to do it."

They sat quietly a moment. Emma felt comforted in some obscure way. She had not wondered consciously whether Molly was into magic herself, but she felt reassured to hear her say emphatically that she was not. "What *do* you believe?" she asked.

Molly's eyes opened wider, and she frowned. She leaned back. "I used to go to this spirituality group. We talked about Tarot, astrology, spiritualism, herbal magic. It was interesting. I used to do Tarot readings, and I believe in astrology."

"Hmm. I'm not sure if I believe in astrology or not. Sometimes it seems to explain things."

Molly nodded and continued, "Well, I'm not religious. I was raised Episcopalian, but now I don't go to any church."

"Episcopalian," Emma said with a small chuckle. "I would have thought Catholic, with the Irish name."

"Nope." Molly smiled. "My parents had a mixed marriage. My mother was the Episcopalian, and she wanted us raised that way. It wasn't nearly as exciting as Catholic. Maybe I would have stayed with it if it had been. Nothing to be afraid of."

"Do you like to be afraid?"

Molly looked surprised. "Well, maybe a little. I like scary movies. Suspense, not slasher. How about you?"

Emma drew a deep breath. "I'm rational, mostly. But I think that it's best not to mess around with the supernatural. You never know what might happen." She felt almost apologetic before such a direct question. "I used to be interested in goddess religion. I went to a few feminist spirituality circles. But it didn't touch me the way it did some people. I look at goddess worship like any other supernatural system—as myths, stories, and rituals that originate in the human mind. I believe myths tell us about ourselves, and a story tells the hidden truth, the bones under mere facts."

Molly was looking at her, lips slightly smiling. Emma felt suddenly embarrassed and wished she hadn't talked so much. "But you haven't told me what you believe—other than astrology."

Molly looked up at the blue morning sky peeking through a dogwood's late summer leaves. She looked back at Emma. "I believe in nature. And in love."

Emma felt her face grow hot. "Love," she said in a low voice. "That's not always easy to believe in."

"That's a fact," Molly said. "But I keep trying." She wiped her mouth and stood. "You want to come over and look at the catalog?"

CHAPTER 17
Dogs and Books

Max Heindel, Simplified Scientific Astrology: A Complete Textbook on the Art of Erecting a Horoscope, *1954, green cloth with gilt illustrations and embossing on front cover and gilt lettering on spine. How to cast a horoscope and different aspects of astrology. Includes a glossary and illustrations of charts and tables.*

Pulling up in front of Molly's bungalow, the first thing Emma noticed was the front window, where two large, long-faced dogs were looking out at her. When she got out of the car, she could hear their sharp barks, like a call and response in some canine church, and the scrabbles and thuds of their paws on the glass. As the women approached the porch, the hounds started howling.

"There's the welcoming party," Molly said.

Emma was a little cautious about entering a house with such large, energetic dogs. A massive oak cast shade over the front yard, and it felt ten degrees cooler than the street. She lingered by the garden that took up most of the yard. It was full of shade plants. Many she knew—hostas, hellebores, and ferns, but Molly pointed out toad lilies, trillium, and a vast array of epimedium, heucheras, and a massive Japanese anemone. What had looked at her first glance like a mass of foliage became a wild garden with loosely defined areas. She was drawn to the dark-reds, purples, and improbably bright lime green of the heucheras.

As they approached the door, Molly said, "Wait here a minute. I'll put up the guys."

Emma was relieved. She didn't like dogs jumping on her, and one of those beasts could probably knock over someone her size. After what seemed like five minutes, Molly swung the door open. They went into a parlor with built-in bookshelves, obviously not nearly enough, as there were a variety of other bookshelves against the walls with books stacked high above. One poor bookshelf had books stacked on top that equaled the height of the bookshelf itself. Emma caught a whiff of dog and noticed a few clumps of dog hair on the floor.

Molly picked up a washcloth that was in the hallway. "Blavatsky has a passion for washcloths. I don't know where she finds them."

Through an arched doorway, they entered the dining room. More stacks of books lay on the large mahogany dining table, along with rolls of Mylar, bubble wrap, and scissors. Molly pushed the supplies to one end of the table, and they sat side by side near the cleared-away area. Emma told herself she could never live like that. She liked having everything in its place, and she usually put away supplies right after using them.

Molly spread the catalog open. "Do you want to go through it page by page, or should I just show you what I circled?"

"Do you really have to ask? I want to see *A Boke of Secret Knowlege!*"

Molly grinned impishly. "Of course," she said,

flipping right to it and handing the catalog to Emma.

Emma read out loud: "'323. Anon., *A Boke of Secret Knowlege by A Learned Doctor.* Handwritten manuscript. Leaves, held together by ribbon, not bound. No Date, circa 16th—17th century. Astrology, demonology, fortune-telling, and divers subjects of interest to the curious and the neophyte practitioner. Second half is a grimoire.'"

The two women looked at each other.

Emma said, "I wish I hadn't mailed that book. I want to look at it again for his description."

"But this description doesn't mention the note. We've got to see this manuscript and compare the paper and writing to the note."

"How?"

"Simple. I've picked out a few books that I'd like to add to my stock if the price is right. And there are other books that are candidates for the warning note. I'll call Dr. Booth and ask him if I can buy a few of the books, but I'd like to see the condition beforehand."

"When?"

"You want to go with me?"

"Yes. Just say I'm your partner." As soon as she said it, Emma felt embarrassed. She hastily added, "Like Jay and Harry are partners. Book partners."

Molly seemed to take no notice of the double meaning, to Emma's relief. She was focused on the catalog. "I do want to go over this list once more to make sure I haven't missed anything or to rule out some of the books I circled." She smoothed the catalog to make it lie flat. "I don't know—he gave me a week. If I call the very next day, will he think I'm too eager and give a high price?"

"No telling. I didn't meet him, but if it were me, I

might think I was sitting on a gold mine. On the other hand, he might not keep his word and will mail the catalog to the specialists he found without waiting. I'm not sure I trust him."

"Well, won't hurt to give him a call. Want to go over the list with me?"

They bent their heads and started on page one with Alchemy. By the time they finished going over Magic (Black), Emma stretched and rolled her head around in circles. She looked at her watch and saw that it was two-thirty-three. Molly asked, "Want some lunch?"

Emma knew she should go home or at least say she should go. Molly might think she was outstaying her welcome. But the catalog was fascinating. She felt like she was getting an education on a subject matter she never thought she would be interested in. "Lunch would be great." She followed Molly into the kitchen. Since the dogs were shut up in a bedroom close by, they started barking.

"Come meet the dogs," Molly said. Emma was a little wary, but since Molly obviously doted on them so much, she felt she couldn't possibly refuse.

"It's okay, guys." When they saw Molly, their tails wagged as though the tail controlled the whole dog. Blavatsky and Dmitri each had their own huge crate with a food bowl, a water bowl, and a sleeping bag to lie on. They barked sharply, and Emma backed away. She had a dread of sudden, loud noises. She stayed in the doorway while Molly went toward their crates.

Both were white with black and tan spots. Dmitri was a little larger than Blavatsky and had more black on his body. Blavatsky watched Molly's every move, her tail going around in circles. Molly reached into a bag, pulled out a strong-smelling piece of fake bacon, and gave one to each. Dmitri held it in his paws to eat it, but Blavatsky gobbled hers down. As they ate, Molly crooned to them a little song about dogs getting something good. When they had finished with their treats, they looked up expectantly, smiles on their faces.

Emma said weakly, "Hello, dogs." Molly nodded approval. Emma stepped cautiously to Blavatsky's crate and said, "Hi, girl. How's the good dog?"

She was rewarded by a low growl.

"I think she doesn't like me," Emma said, stepping back.

"She has to get used to you."

Emma turned to the other dog and said, "How's the fellow?" The dog smiled and pawed at the door of his cage, tail wagging merrily. He gave a small whine. "I think this one might like me," Emma said.

"Dmitri loves everybody," Molly said. "Don't you, good little sweet little boy?"

"Little? They each probably weigh as much as I do." When Dmitri stood, Emma noticed the deep chest and narrow hips. "They look like hairier, bigger greyhounds."

"They're related to greyhounds," Molly said. "The real name of the breed is Borzoi, but I like the Russian Wolfhound name. Actually, they have a little German Shepherd in them, so they are more energetic and territorial than other wolfhounds. Of course, I didn't realize it until they came to live with me."

After they had paid their respects to the dogs, Molly and Emma went into Molly's kitchen and closed the door. Emma was pleased to see how large it was but looked askance at the unwashed dishes in the sink and on the counter.

"How about a grilled cheese sandwich?" asked

Molly.

Emma usually had a salad for lunch, but she agreed. She was glad to see the loaf of whole-grain bread that Molly pulled out, as well as the chunk of unsliced cheddar. No pre-sliced, processed cheese, thank goodness. And real butter went into the skillet. When Molly took out two root beers from the fridge, her satisfaction was complete. She had learned to drink root beer in New York and loved its oddly bubble-gum-like taste.

They sat at the kitchen counter and ate their sandwiches. Molly kept up a line of small talk, mostly about book dealers and their foibles. Emma looked around the kitchen. It looked well used, like a kitchen that someone actually cooked in. Actually, the whole house was set up for one person and that person's interests, like her own house with its many crammed-full bookshelves. Molly's clutter was working clutter. Some of the books and knickknacks were covered with dust, and Emma longed to take a dust cloth to them. But she told herself that people live differently.

"So the plan is," Molly said, "I'll call Dr. Booth and go over there, list of books in hand, and ask him if we can look at the books we circled." She smiled at Emma, her blue eyes sparkling. "Are you free tomorrow?"

Emma nodded. "I'll have to check my calendar, but I think so." She pulled out a leatherette notebook and, after flipping through it, nodded.

As Molly negotiated with Dr. Booth over the phone, Emma listened, but could only hear half of the conversation.

When Molly ended the call, she said, "I told Dr. Booth that I was interested in about twenty of the books, but I wanted to come over and check out the condition before making an offer. At first, he didn't want to sell any of them separately from the others. He implied he'd talked to someone who was interested in the entire collection. He said there were about two thousand books, and he could sell them at a better price as a collection. But we talked a bit more, and he came around and said I could have ten of them, no more. 'I don't want them divided up piecemeal, blah, blah.' I said I would narrow down my list when I actually saw the books and what condition they're in. So we're going over tomorrow afternoon at three. Is that okay? And before you go home, do you want me to take the dogs out of their crates so you can pet them?"

Emma hesitated.

Molly's mouth twitched with the start of an impish grin. "I saw you glancing at my sink. Do you want to do my dishes?"

Flustered, Emma blurted out, "Yes! I mean, No, no, yes. Ah, I mean yes, no, no."

Molly began to laugh. After a moment, Emma laughed, too.

As the women laughed, the two dogs joined in, joyfully barking in call and response.

CHAPTER 18
Wall of Books

Israel Regardie, The Golden Dawn: An Account of the Teaching, Rites, and Ceremonies of the Hermetic Order of the Golden Dawn. *Four volumes, 1937—1940. Black cloth with gilt lettered spine. Explanation of magical and kabalistic theory with instructions for initiation rituals, invisibility and shape-shifting rituals, and how to use Tarot, astrology, and more.*

Once again, Molly stood with Emma looking at the wall of books in Dr. Booth's basement. After showing them in, the dentist instructed them not to take too long because he had to pick up his daughter soon.

"I'll go along the rows, pick out the books I've chosen, and pile them up here," Molly said to Emma. "Would you look for the grimoires? I listed the ones that say they were printed before 1610. Make sure they aren't reprints." She did not want to buy grimoires, but wanted to see which of them the note could have been inserted into. But she suspected *A Boke of Secret Knowlege* was the one.

"Okay." Emma started looking along the lowest shelf first. Molly watched her, gray-streaked hair swinging in front of her face as she sat on the floor to peruse the books. She wondered how old Emma was.

Molly had to use the rickety ladder more than once to bring down books from the top shelf. But she soon saw that they were shelved alphabetically within each category, so she had little trouble finding the books on her list. Many of them were in bad condition: hinges broken, moldy, marred by silverfish. Such a pretty name for a creepy insect that leaves its egg sac on the top edges of book pages!

She descended the ladder and sat cross-legged on the floor to separate her preferred books from the others. Emma came up with about four books in her hands.

"Here are the grimoires," Emma said, setting them down. One was the manuscript in the clamshell box that Molly had looked at before. The others were printed and bound.

"Only one manuscript?" asked Molly, picking it up.

"It's the *Lesser Key*. But I can't find *A Boke of Secret Knowlege*."

"What?" Molly looked at her. "Are you sure? It's on the list right after *Lesser Key*."

"Yes, but I couldn't find it on the shelves. And I looked. I climbed the ladder, I got down on my knees on that hard concrete floor to read spines, I pulled manuscripts out of the shelves and had the worst time trying to keep some of them together, they're so fragile. But it isn't here."

"That means that Buck must have taken it."

"If so, the police probably have it."

Molly let out an exasperated sigh. "Well, let's look at the other manuscript and see if the paper and time period match the note. If not, that will rule it out."

Calendarium Naturale Magicum Perpetuum was

handprinted on vellum with cloth ties and appeared to be about the same time as the note. So this book was a possibility if the note could have slipped from the ties.

They each took one book at a time to check the time period and contents. The first was *Ars Goetia* that contained the demon's seals and how to invoke them, but on close examination, it appeared to be an early 20th century reprint of the 1608 edition. Unless the signer of the warning was someone other than Simon Forman, that one would not be contemporary with the note. Magical spells were in each of the remaining books—for finding lost objects, protecting one's home from evil, and so forth—but none seemed particularly demonic.

"So *A Boke of Secret Knowlege* is missing. And it seems to be the most likely suspect for where the warning page originated." Molly smiled a crooked smile. "What a happenstance that you felt the urge to steal that book."

"I prefer to call it borrowing without the owner's permission," Emma said primly. "But we don't have it now."

"Maybe you can find another copy," Molly said.

"I know! I'll look online to see if any universities have it."

"Good. You pursue that, and I'm going to look online for *A Boke of Secret Knowlege*."

They looked through the bookcase until Dr. Booth came downstairs and said he had to go pick up his daughter from her dance lesson.

"There is one book that I'm interested in that we can't find," Molly said. "Do you know where this one could be?" She pointed to the catalog listing.

Dr. Booth gave the list a quick glance. "No idea. I

never came down here until after he died. Granddad never let us come downstairs. Said the stairs were too dangerous."

"Okay. If it shows up, please let me know." She indicated her stack of ten books. "How much are the ten I selected?"

He glanced at the stack. "How about $50 each?"

"What?"

He shrugged. "Make me an offer."

"How about $250 for all of them?" She knew some would retail for over $200 since she had looked them up. But they might take a long time to sell. The cheaper ones were hardly worth $50.

"You halved my offer?" He frowned. "Why don't we split the difference? $375?"

Molly pretended to consider and then said, "Sounds good. Since we're here, do you think we could look upstairs? We didn't have a chance to go through the whole house."

"Didn't you hear me say I had to pick up my daughter?"

"I'm sorry. I forgot. Let me write you a check." She didn't dare ask if they could return.

As they walked away, Molly wondered whether she was wrong or practical not to offer to buy all the books.

She felt happily consoled when Emma suggested they go to Oxygen. It was still daylight, so they sat outside. The whippet was there again. Since it was nearly suppertime, Emma ordered white wine, and Molly ordered a stout. They each got a caprese sandwich.

"I should bring Blavatsky and Dmitri here sometime," said Molly.

"I bet they'll love it." Emma didn't sound like she wanted to be included.

After they finished their sandwiches, each woman turned to her mobile device. Molly looked for *A Boke of Secret Knowlege* while Emma looked for *Against the Diabolical*.

Molly looked on viaLibri and other websites and found no copies for sale, so she went to World Cat, the online database for world-wide library holdings, which didn't show any copies. The *Boke* belonging to Dr. Booth must be unique.

Emma seemed absorbed in her phone. Suddenly she looked up, eyes gleaming. "Candler University has a copy of Lewis's book in Special Collections. I'll go and look at it first thing tomorrow."

CHAPTER 19
All His Rarities

Benedict Williamson, Supernatural Mysticism, *1921, dark blue cloth with gilt on spine. A Catholic priest's look at mysticism for the layman.*

Emma loved the old part of the library at Candler. She had researched an article there once and remembered the overwhelming sense of nostalgia mixed with anticipation as she walked through the quiet stacks, with their faint smell of time-weathered pages and bindings.

The ground floor and the floor above it were all new. The media area was round, white-painted, and full of light, with computers set about in circular and curved arrangements. She quickly found a seat and pulled up RAMBL, the catalog of rare books, manuscripts, and papers held by the university. She found *Against the Diabolical* and printed its information.

Getting out of the elevator on the floor where Special Collections was housed, she felt a sense of the old Candler library again. High ceilings, dark walls, a hushed quality. She could almost imagine she had gone back in time to Lewis's own youth, visiting a library to find a rare book. Only then there would have been wooden card catalogs, yellowed cards with information typed on them. And she would have been wearing a skirt, hose, and heels, and her hair would have been curled, most likely under a hat. Those were the days. Yeah, right.

After presenting her ID and waiting for her online registration form to be confirmed, Emma at length found herself ensconced in the reading room with *Against the Diabolical* set before her on a table with a set of written instructions and a library employee sitting at another table, watching her not too obviously. She opened the book. It was the same as Fred's except that the limited edition letter on this copy was B. She knew that didn't mean it was more valuable than Fred's letter K, but seeing it still gave her a small thrill. And she felt a leap of excitement when she saw that this one was signed. She traced the signature with her forefinger and felt a moment's warmth for this man whose writings had stimulated, excited, warmed, frustrated, and angered her for so long. She remembered reading *The Lion, the Witch, and the Wardrobe* as a child. She had not realized it was a Christian allegory until much later, but by then it had passed into her imagination like an enzyme, coloring it from that day forward. She shook her head and turned to the introduction again. She read it over carefully, searching for anything that might have mentioned a warning. Suddenly she exclaimed aloud, "Ah-hah!"

The librarian looked at her. Emma mouthed, "Sorry."

Lewis recounted how his student placed his hand over the demon's picture and said, "What follows is only for the initiated."

Emma read the lines over a few times. What follows

is only for the initiated. She picked up the photocopied note that read: *Whosoever readeth this boke without leave of the Circle, let him BEWARE. SF.*

Lewis didn't mention a warning note, but he did mention a loose sheet of paper. Maybe that sheet was the warning note. You'd think a warning would be at the front of the book. But on the other hand, if the first part was about astrology, alchemy, and divination, maybe the warning page was placed later in the book. After all, Mr. Booth's catalog had said that the second half was a grimoire.

She leafed through the book again in a desultory way. She stopped, all attention. Inserted in the back was a laid-in library note that read, "See Alfred Bartholomew James Harford, Seventh Lord Agerton, 1913-33."

She took out her tablet and researched Lord Agerton. This particular Alfred Bartholomew Harford was mentioned in an article about the family's ancestral home in Buckinghamshire. It was now open to the public with the latest Lord and Lady Agerton living in small quarters in the original castle tower built by the Normans. After Alfred's death, the title went to his brother, grandfather of the current Lord Agerton. Was this a dead end? What happened to the manuscript? She put in a search for *A Boke of Secret Knowlege* along with Lord Agerton. To her delight, she quickly found a dissertation called "C.S. Lewis: Christianity and the Diabolical in The Narnia Books, *The Space Trilogy*, and *Against the Diabolical*." And the dissertation was housed at Candler.

Emma immediately requested to see the dissertation. While waiting, she did a Google search for the author, Shirley Parnell, and discovered that she was a professor of Religion at the Candler School of Theology. Since the university's directory included office phone numbers of faculty members, Emma found and wrote down Professor Parnell's number. Maybe, just maybe, the professor would know about the manuscript and even who the author was. But even if Simon Forman wrote the note, did that prove him to be the author of *A Boke of Secret Knowlege*?

When the dissertation was delivered to her table, she turned to the chapter entitled "C. S. Lewis's Colleague and His Mysterious 'Boke.'" The author claimed that Lewis's colleague was Alfred Harford, Lord Agerton. Skimming the chapter, she read that the manuscript owned by young Lord Agerton must have been sold at auction when the family's library was auctioned off in the 1970's. Maggs Brothers in London acquired most of the items, but no copy of the auction catalog was to be found. Emma's breath quickened. This type of elusive paper trail thrilled her. She put a "wanted to buy" item on her email booksellers listserv for the Maggs Brothers catalog or the auction catalog of the estate sale of Agerton. She felt a touch of smugness. Academic researchers often were not aware of research resources that booksellers employed.

Emma stepped outside the reading room, telling the attendant she needed to make a call. In the ladies' room, she called Dr. Parnell and got her voice mail.

"Dr. Parnell, my name is Emma Clarke. I'm interested in Simon Forman and am reading the chapter in your dissertation on the provenance of *A Boke of Secret Knowlege*. I'd be very interested in discussing it with you if you have some time. You can reach me at—" Emma gave her number and email.

Emma went home with a million thoughts running through her head about estate sales at castles and Lord

Agerton's untimely death. Lewis wouldn't say how his student died. Was it a disease, accident, suicide? Was the manuscript even in the sale? Or did the family keep it? Or was it left in Oxford when his family packed up all his belongings?

It was after ten, but she knew Molly stayed up late. She called her, but got her voice mail.

After leaving Molly a message, she picked up her copy of Rowse's book on Simon Forman and began to look through it. As she recalled, Forman had written over forty manuscripts about astrology, medicine, and magic, some sounding rather dark. In 1590, he had written a book that contained instructions for "calling spirits good and evil." Rowse insisted that Simon never practiced black magic, which Rowse defined as "for the purpose of inflicting evil." How could you call evil spirits without the possibility of inflicting evil? And why would you call them anyway? Just for the fun of it? Maybe that was what Lord Agerton and his friends were doing. A thrilling lark, with a bit of sex and bondage thrown in.

Reading along and nodding, suddenly Emma sat up, startled. Simon had, in fact, practiced necromancy, according to Rowse. He had gone somewhere to attend a circle to raise spirits and had heard unearthly music. Another time, he had heard "piping of the fairies." And in October 1597, he wrote that a spirit appeared in fire and that he smelled fire and brimstone, but he did not see the spirit, only "a kind of shape."

Power of suggestion? On All Hallows Eve, Simon and someone else went again to raise the spirit. Once more, Simon said he did not see the spirit, but heard him speak. On the second of November, the spirit came again, and they "bound him strongly until almost four o'clock in the morning." Bound with what? Spells?

Simon Forman (she read) had bequeathed his manuscripts to his friend and colleague, Richard Napier, who was also an astrologer. Rowse quoted: "All his rarities, secret manuscripts, of what quality soever, Dr. Napier of Lindford in Buckinghamshire had." *Buckinghamshire? Where Lord Agerton's family castle is?* Emma's heart beat faster.

All his rarities. Would those rarities have included *A Boke of Secret Knowlege by a Learned Doctor*?

Simon published one book out of all his voluminous manuscripts: *The Grounds of the Longitude,* about calculating latitudes and longitudes for purposes of sea voyages. He was mysterious about it, saying that the problem of longitude was to be found by a secret way: "unknown to those to whom myself have showed it. They that do know it are sworn by a sacred oath not to manifest the same without leave of the Author." That had a ring of the warning note: "without leave of the Circle."

Dr. Napier left Forman's manuscripts to his nephew, also named Richard Napier, also a doctor and astrologer. The younger Napier gave them to Elias Ashmole, who included Simon's papers in his own vast collection donated to the Bodleian Library. Simon's book on summoning spirits good and evil was in the Bodleian, classified as Ashmole Ms. 244.

Emma stretched. Her mind was spinning, it was late, and Molly still hadn't called her back. She wanted to go to bed, but she thought she would first do a search on Simon Forman. On her first try, she pulled up a website with a picture of the astrologer, the same as on the cover of Rowse's book. With his intense eyes and wild hair, he looked the very stereotype of a mad wizard.

Scrolling down the page, Emma stopped. A graphic showed Forman's signature, large and clear. Emma stared at it and picked up the photocopy of the warning note. The "S" and "F" in both the web picture and the note looked almost identical.

Was *A Boke of Secret Knowlege* really by Simon Forman? Had it been in the Ashmole collection? If it had been, had someone stolen it from the Bodleian? Or maybe it had never been in the Ashmole collection at all. Maybe it was kept out for some reason by one of the Napiers or by Ashmole. Maybe it somehow got passed down through the generations until it came into the hands of Lewis's young friend at Oxford, whom Professor Parnell believed was Alfred Bartholomew James Harford, Seventh Lord Agerton.

Emma needed to talk to Professor Parnell. And even more, she needed to talk to Molly.

CHAPTER 20
Planning Something Legal This Time

Arthur Conan Doyle, The New Revelation, *1918, black cloth with gilt on spine. Doyle's studies into psychical research, especially life after death.*

Molly pulled open the heavy wooden door of Samuel's, a popular in-town tavern where the book fair planners were meeting for lunch. As her eyes quickly adjusted to the dim lighting of the original part of the tavern, she saw dark wood paneling, booths, and people sitting at the bar. The smell of frying onions made her mouth water. She turned left and entered a large room with big, wide windows, full of light, round tables made of dark wood in the center and square tables along the side. Samuel's had built the addition about thirty years ago to accommodate those customers who preferred a more open, daylight-filled place to drink and eat the burgers Samuel's was famous for, and now more leafy options for the health conscious. Customers who preferred the dark, old-style bar atmosphere of the original still hung out in the room with the booths and the bar. Now craft brews and wines supplemented the Buds, PBRs, and Coronas favored by the more traditional crowd. But Samuel's was still a favorite gathering and hobnobbing place for a range of people from political types, to students, to theater folk, to uniformed police officers.

Looking around, Molly saw Jay waving her over to a round table by a window where he and Harry were sitting.

"Hey," Molly said, sliding into a chair and grabbing a menu.

Jay leaned close to Molly. "So who do you think murdered Buck?"

"I don't know." She shrugged. "Who do you suspect?" Jay loved to gossip.

"We-ll," he drawled, leaning closer, a conspiratorial half grin on his face, "I have two theories. First, Emma says she heard a noise and goes downstairs, right?"

Molly nodded.

"Then you go. Remember, I passed you and saw you going toward the basement door. You say Emma and you are the only ones down there. So who is the murderer?" He drew back with an air of pulling a rabbit out of a hat. "Either you—or Emma!"

"Jay!" Molly exclaimed, half amused, half annoyed. "Surely you don't think—"

"Naw, it wasn't you." He grimaced and shook his head. "I doubt you'd kill Buck no matter how mad you got at him. I know you. You're an upstanding citizen." He grinned again. "So it must have been Emma."

"Oh, Jay, that's ridiculous." Molly shook her head and turned her attention to the menu.

Harry leaned toward her, one denim-sleeved elbow propped on the table. His wavy ponytail fell over his shoulder. "How well do you know Emma, anyway?"

Molly scowled at him. "I just met her. But she doesn't seem like a murderer to me." She started to say, "we're friends" but decided not to. The less the booksellers knew, the better. "Emma doesn't seem like a killer," she repeated.

"But maybe she has a temper," said Jay. "People sometimes do things out of blind rage."

"I've never seen her get angry," Molly said. "You said you had two theories. What's the second?"

Fred hurried in, a large folder under his arm. "Sorry I'm late," he said, breathing hard. His round, white-bearded face glowed red like the Coca-Cola Santa's.

The waiter appeared, and they all placed their orders. Molly ordered her favorite: a burger, medium rare, with onion rings. Fred ordered a barbecue sandwich, Harry ordered fish and chips, and Jay got a salad.

After the waiter left, Jay said, "Okay. Emma hears a noise, you hear a noise. You both go to investigate. So where'd the killer go?" His red hair flopped over his forehead.

"I have no idea," Molly said. *Damn,* she thought. *I don't want him to figure out the murder before we do.* "We didn't see anyone down there."

"Is there a hiding place in the basement?" Jay shook his head and pursed his lips. "I walked around the house before the sale, and I didn't see anything that looked like a basement door or a back door. Not up to code, by the way. Odd for such a ritzy neighborhood. So the killer had to come back up the stairs, didn't he?"

Fred interrupted in a gruff voice, "Can we talk about the book fair? I don't have all day."

While Fred gave the book fair's financial report, Molly thought about Jay's theory. She felt unreasonable indignation at his suggestion. How could he suspect Emma? She wouldn't be likely to investigate a murder that she herself had committed. Or would she? Maybe that would be the perfect cover. Molly chomped down on an onion ring and told herself not to be silly. Emma was her friend.

But Molly remembered that she herself had wondered about Emma before getting to know her. Had Emma told her the complete truth about the few minutes she was in the basement before running for help? And why had she opened a door marked "Do Not Enter?" Molly was ninety-nine percent sure it couldn't have been Emma. But her honesty whispered, *what about the other one percent?*

"Molly? Do you have the final cost of the tables?" Fred stared at her.

"Oh. Yes, I do." She brought her mind back to the book fair and pulled out her notebook. She gave her report and wrote down what else she needed to do: call the table rental company and order the tables, look up the cost of table covers and extra chairs, and ask if they got free signs.

After each of them had written down their next tasks, Jay abruptly rose. "Gotta run. Meredith is getting out of school at two."

Molly said, keeping her voice unconcerned, "I didn't hear your second theory."

"You tell her, Harry." Jay threw down some bills, thunked his iced tea glass on the table, spilling a few drops, and sped from the room.

"I have to leave, too," Fred said, shuffling his papers together and taking a final swallow of tea.

Molly was relieved he didn't mention that one of his books was missing. He probably didn't realize yet that it was gone. He wouldn't check his shelves every day to make sure each book was in place. Emma had said she mailed the C.S. Lewis book Friday. What would

Fred think when he received a book of his that he didn't even know was missing?

"So what's the theory, Harry?" she said when they were the only ones left.

"Well," said Harry, leaning closer, "we couldn't figure how someone had time to come back upstairs after Emma came and got you. And since there were no exterior basement doors, it had to be someone who was standing in line and went in at the same time we did, and they must have hid out in the basement. What else could they have done?"

"Right." Molly nodded, keeping her face neutral. All at once she remembered the broom closet under the basement stairs. What if someone had been hiding there while she and Emma were discovering Buck's body? She shivered. But Emma did say she saw the corner of the bookshelf move, so the murderer must have left that way.

"So if we rule out Emma, who's left?" went on Harry. "Most of those who were in line hadn't gone into the house yet, but even if some did, there would still have been twenty-five. Not necessarily the same twenty-five if some had already left. So Jay and I started counting who was in line. A few we didn't know, but there were the usual suspects who get to sales super early. Then we realized when we were all out in the yard being questioned by the cops, one person was missing: Michael."

"Who?"

"You know, that engineer who collects presidential stuff. He usually goes through all the books, so it's unlikely he was done."

Molly nodded, relieved. They were going in an entirely different direction from her and Emma, thank goodness.

Harry continued, "Maybe he got mad when he saw Buck go downstairs and they got into a fight or something. You know they have a history."

Molly said, "Or maybe he left early because there was nothing he wanted."

Harry shrugged. "That's possible." He took a sip of iced tea. "And it also might have been one of the other people in line that we didn't know. I wish I had counted how many people were in the yard when the cops were there."

"Good thought." She ate the last onion ring. "The police would know how many were interviewed since they questioned everyone who was still there."

"Anyway, Jay and I, we think Michael is the most logical suspect."

"You may be right. I don't remember him in the yard either after the police got there." She was glad he had a plausible suspect besides Emma.

They walked out into the glaring sun, more glaring now since they'd been within the wood-paneled walls of Samuel's. Apropos of nothing, Molly thought of the film noir movies where the cops shone a large light into the suspect's eyes. *How many suspects are there?* she wondered.

CHAPTER 21
Call Me

Francois Lenormant, Chaldean Magic: Its Origin and Development, *1877, green cloth cover with black lettering and an illustration of a dog or a demon on front, gilt lettering and symbols on spine. Magical practices of the Chaldeans of ancient Assyria, based on the translation of a large tablet from Nineveh, containing incantations against evil spirits, the effects of sorcery, and disease.*

Molly sat on the sofa with her feet on the coffee table strewn with magazines and catalogs that she never ordered from. Dmitri was stretched out beside her with his head and front paws on her lap, while Blavatsky was in the easy chair she had claimed for her own. Dmitri wouldn't dare try to get on it. Molly was reading yesterday's paper since she liked to keep up with the political columnists. She tested herself to see if she ever agreed with the conservatives, even a little. Halfway through George Will, her phone rang.

"Hi, Emma." She felt unexpected joy bubble up at the sound of Emma's voice.

"Molly!" Emma's voice sounded irritated. "I left

you a message last night and again this morning. Why didn't you call me back? I've got news."

Molly felt deflated. "I listened to your message, but I thought it might be too late to call. I know you go to bed early. I got up late and had to rush to meet Jay and Harry and Fred for lunch, to talk about the book fair we're planning."

"You could have at least texted this morning." Emma's voice still sounded annoyed.

"I said, I had to meet Jay and Harry and Fred for—"

"Fred? Did he mention the Lewis book?"

"Nope. All he wanted to talk about was the book fair. As a matter of fact, Jay and I were talking about the murder and he interrupted us."

"Well, how rude!" Emma said, voice tinged with sarcasm. "Especially since that is what you were meeting about, wasn't it—the book fair?"

"Yeah," Molly said, ignoring the sarcasm. "But a little conversation off-topic enlivens every meeting." Molly stroked Dmitri's head. "So Jay and Harry have a theory about the murderer."

"What?" Emma's voice sounded impatient.

Molly sure wasn't going to tell her about theory number one, that Emma herself was a suspect, especially in the mood she was in. "They think the killer had to be one of the first twenty-five that were let into the house, and that they hid in the basement."

"Like *Murder on the Orient Express* or one of those closed-house mysteries."

"Yeah. They were speculating about Michael, who was at the front of the line, but he wasn't in the yard when the police questioned us. And he and Buck don't get along. Hey, wait a minute. He's the one who helped Maisie into the house, remember? I suppose it's possible that he did it."

"Ha! He helps an elderly woman on a walker, then commits cold-blooded murder minutes later! Did you tell them anything about our investigation?"

"Nope! I just wanted to hear what they were thinking."

"So do you want to hear *my* news?" Emma said, her voice still sharp.

"Sure."

"I went to the Candler Library to the Rare Books Reading Room to see their copy of *Against the Diabolical*. And you'll never guess what was in it!"

"What?"

"A library note, a cross-reference to someone named Alfred Lord Agerton. Died young, at age twenty, and his dates would have made him the right age to have been at Oxford in the early 1930's. I looked him up, and it turns out there's a Candler professor who wrote her dissertation about C. S. Lewis and the diabolical, including the mysterious manuscript. And—she believes that this Lord Agerton was Lewis's student!"

"Wow!"

"That's not all. When I went home, I researched more about Simon Forman. It seems he was into necromancy and summoning spirits. He claims to have been in a circle and heard a spirit talking. He said they bound the spirit for several hours."

"Double wow!"

"That might not have been considered black magic according to the beliefs of the time," Emma said, "since he didn't say anything about harming anyone. But he was in a circle, and the word "circle" is used in the warning note."

"Right," Molly said.

"And that's not all." Emma's words tumbled out. "I went online and found a replica of his signature. The capital letters—the "S" and the "F"—look the same as in that note you found. That means Simon is—or is very likely to be—the author of the *Boke*."

"I want to see that signature!" Molly said. Mentally, she kicked herself. She ought to have known what Simon Forman's signature looked like if it was out there online for everyone to see.

"Go to *astrologersearlymodern.com*," Emma said. "It's right there on the home page." She told Molly about Simon Forman and how his papers came to be in the Bodleian. "And there's more," she said. "One of Forman's manuscripts in the Bodleian is about calling good and evil spirits! It's Ashmole 244."

"So that means Forman did write at least one manuscript about calling evil spirits," breathed Molly.

"Right," Emma said. "Another thing: Forman published only one book and put a warning in it, saying that only those who had the leave of the author were allowed to read it."

"Testifies to his secrecy, if nothing else."

"Doesn't the language sound familiar?"

"It does. 'Leave of the author' and 'leave of the Circle.'"

"So I'm thinking two things," Emma continued. "One, that our missing manuscript, *A Boke of Secret Knowlege*, is by Forman; and, two, that it's the same manuscript Lewis's friend had."

They were both quiet a moment.

"So I gave the Candler professor, Dr. Parnell, a call asking to discuss her dissertation," Emma said. "I'm waiting for her to call me back."

"Wait a minute," Molly said. "You've already read

this dissertation? Has the professor actually seen *A Boke of Secret Knowlege?*"

"It doesn't say," Emma said.

"And Grandpa Booth had it on his shelf all this time," Molly said, shaking her head. "When you talk to her, don't tell her that you know that *A Boke* was in the Booth collection, and that now it's gone. Don't tell her anything."

"Why not?" asked Emma.

"I don't want anyone else to know what we're doing. Not yet. Why don't you just say that you read the Lewis book and you're interested in the manuscript."

"I'll ask her if she read the *Boke* herself."

"Okay. But don't give her any more information. I don't think we need to tell this professor any more than she knows already."

"Very well, I won't tell her. I'll try to find out what she knows."

CHAPTER 22
Fruitless or Not?

Q. K. Philander Doesticks, The Witches of New York, *1858, brown blind stamped cover with gilt lettering on spine. Pseudonym of Mortimer Thompson, a journalist who traveled around New York City talking to witches.*

Professor Parnell was not what Emma expected. Fiftyish, with carefully coiffed blonde hair and high heels, she greeted Emma with, "Ms. Clarke?"

"Doctor Emma Clarke," Emma said smoothly.

"Please have a seat." Parnell's smile was formal, not inviting. She gestured to a wooden chair and seated herself behind her desk with an air of rigid waiting.

"Thank you, Dr. Parnell." Emma sat in the hard chair. She could see behind the professor a tall bookshelf with a row of books by Lewis and a set of reference books. The *Catholic Encyclopedia*?

"I'm interested in C.S. Lewis," Emma said, "and I came across your dissertation recently. Could I ask you a few questions?"

"I have a meeting in half an hour." The professor looked at her watch.

"I won't keep you long. I was wondering whether

you have learned more about Lord Agerton, and if he was really Lewis's student at Oxford."

Dr. Parnell shook her head. "I didn't find out anything more about Agerton. He was not significant to my research."

"Did you ever find out how he died?"

Parnell hesitated. "No. Why are you interested?"

"I thought it might add more to what we know about Lewis. Particularly why he was so adamantly against any sort of alternative or pagan spirituality."

"Lewis was a Christian," said Parnell, as though explaining the obvious to a not very bright student. "To him, what you call alternative or pagan spirituality was wrong, evil, forbidden." Her voice sounded even and controlled.

Emma nodded. "But—did he ever have any experiences with—pagan spirituality—that might have influenced him?"

"Why would he have to have any experiences? Can't we accept that certain people hold strong convictions without having to psychologize those convictions away?"

"Of course they can," Emma said. She refrained from adding *I wasn't psychologizing! Although maybe that is a difference between a religion professor and an English professor: we want to know how writers' experiences influence their writing.* Instead, she said, "Did you ever find out more about *A Boke of Secret Knowlege*? Are there any ideas about who wrote it? Who the "Learned Doctor" might have been?"

"No. I know nothing more about it." Parnell's face was a mask and her voice flat.

"Did you try to find out *where* it was, or if it still exists?" Emma persisted, feeling as though she were trying to roll a stone uphill.

Parnell's face remained expressionless but for her sharp, light green eyes. "No, I said I didn't." She glanced again at her watch. "Now, would you please excuse me? As I said, I have a meeting."

Emma stood. "Thank you for your time, Dr. Parnell."

Parnell stood and came around her desk. "I'm sorry your visit turned out to be a disappointment."

"That's all right," Emma said, resolute and chipper. "Thanks again."

The professor followed as though she were herding Emma out the door. "Goodbye, Dr. Clarke."

On a sudden impulse, Emma turned. "What if the manuscript happened to turn up in Atlanta?"

Parnell's head jerked up, eyes suddenly bright. "Why do you say that?"

Emma shrugged. "I just wondered."

"It's impossible." Parnell shut the door so hard it banged into the metal frame.

Emma stood in the hall, staring at the closed office door. *Well,* she thought. *That was fruitless. Or was it?*

CHAPTER 23
Let's Meet at Our Place

E. D. Walker, Reincarnation, *1916, brown cloth with gilt lettering. Discussion of reincarnation in different societies, including views of authors and poets.*

Molly mused about Jay's and Harry's suspicions. She realized that if those two suspected Emma, the police might suspect her as well. *I should have told her,* she thought. And Michael. She didn't remember seeing him when they returned to pick up books. As an online bookseller, he should have stayed longer, at least looked at all the books.

She turned her thoughts to Ashmole 244. Emma had said that it included the calling of angels and demons. Oh, how Molly longed to go to Oxford and see this manuscript for herself! Surely it would shed light on the *Boke*. She searched online for 244, but all she found was a mention in a footnote of another book, written by a lucky writer who *did* get to go to the Bodleian and ask for 244. Unfortunately, the Bodleian did not digitize its holdings. Since it had all books printed in the UK, such a project would take forever.

If *A Boke of Secret Knowlege* was written by Simon Forman, and it wasn't in the Bodleian, who had held onto it?

Her phone rang, bringing her back to the here and now. It was Emma. Remembering their last phone conversation, Molly suggested they meet for coffee.

"Our place?" Emma asked, a laugh in her voice.

"Yes," Molly said, grinning. "See you shortly." She wondered if she should take Batsky or Dmitri and decided against it. She wanted to stay in Emma's good graces.

There was a pleasant breeze, so they sat outside on a long picnic table bench. Three women sat at the other end, not talking, but staring at their small screens. Emma was wearing a striped top and tight jeans with those ballet flats again.

Molly felt a little nervous and wasn't sure why. She sipped her carmelatto and listened while Emma told about her meeting with Dr. Parnell. "So," Emma ended, "I think she might know more than she's letting on."

"She sounds like a cold water cod," Molly said. "Peculiar."

"I know. Her face stayed completely without expression until, on impulse, I asked her what if the manuscript turned up in Atlanta. Her eyes positively glistened, and she asked why I said that. Then she said it was impossible and almost slammed the door in my face."

"But—if she were truly uninterested, her eyes wouldn't have lit up like that."

"That's why I think she was lying. I feel she knows more than she wants to let on, to me anyway." Emma had her cup of Earl Grey pressed against her lips without drinking, as though smelling the bergamot.

Molly asked, "So do you think she knows where *A Boke* is?"

"Either she knows, or she's really anxious to find out."

"Do you think she might be—?"

"She might be a member of whatever group or circle or coven meets in that ritual room." Emma put her teacup down on top of her spoon, but grabbed it before it could tip over. A few drops of tea splashed out. "I strongly suspect she's involved in black magic."

"But she's a religion professor!" Molly said.

"It's not that incompatible," Emma said. "I know an ordained Unitarian minister who's also a Wiccan priestess. And I used to have a devout Catholic friend who had past life regressions. Religion and magic are closely related. Not usually black magic, though." Emma leaned forward. "So if she is part of the circle— Oh my god, the Circle! What does the note say about the Circle?"

Molly didn't have the note with her but had memorized it. "*'Whosoever readeth this boke without leave of the Circle—'*"

"What if the Circle is the same one that has been meeting in Grandpa Booth's basement?"

"A Circle that has been in existence since Simon Forman's time?"

"Seems improbable, doesn't it?"

Molly's mind was whirring. "So the killer may be one of the Circle? Are we nuts?"

Emma frowned. "I think we're onto something. And I think we ought to tell Detective DuBois."

Molly said, "But if we tell her, she may think we are cuckoo. And how can we tell her without revealing that we were in that room? Which means that we were breaking and entering at worst, or compromising the crime scene, or at the very least trespassing. No, we can't tell her. And anyway, we don't have a suspect. Only a cranky professor who wrote a dissertation decades ago."

"But her reaction!" Emma exclaimed.

"That's no proof of anything." Molly shook her head.

"So maybe it isn't one of the other booksellers."

"Or *you*, Emma."

"What!?" Emma burst out. The women engrossed in their phones looked up for a moment. Then in unison, they tossed back their long hair and resumed looking down.

Molly shrugged. "Jay and Harry have you as their number one suspect. I didn't want to tell you because it was so ludicrous."

"I hope you told them! I don't want the other booksellers thinking about me like that. And if I did, I wouldn't get someone to go back down there with me."

"I have only your word for it," Molly said in a bantering tone, her one percent doubt pushing her. She felt rejection for a moment that Emma had said "someone" and not "you."

Emma opened her mouth and shut it. "Well, if you can't take my word, then why are we sitting here?" She reached down to the floor for her purse and clutched it with both fisted hands. Her black brows almost met. Her mouth was a straight, angry line.

"Emma!" Molly said. "I'm kidding."

"Do you really think for a moment that I might—that I might kill somebody? And then meet with you and talk about it, cool as ice cream? Do you not trust me?" Her face flushed.

Now they had the attention of the phone readers. Molly needed to de-escalate this fast. "Emma, I trust you," she said. "And I sure as shit don't suspect you. And I told Harry and Jay that there was no way you could have done it. I thought you'd think it was funny."

"How would you feel if someone thought you'd murdered someone?"

"I'd laugh."

"Laughing Woman, that's you," said Emma.

"And you're Serious Woman," answered Molly.

"Yes. Sometimes I'm too serious, I admit it." Emma's tight shoulders relaxed a little. A slow smile crept over her still-pink face. She looked down. With her other arm extended, she traced a finger over the handle of her teacup.

Molly reached out and touched the other woman's arm through the thin, striped, cotton knit. She wanted to touch the skin below where the three-quarter-length sleeve ended. Emma's forearm had tiny dark hairs amongst light freckles.

"So," said Molly, giving Emma's arm a slight squeeze. "We can rule you out as a suspect?"

"We can. We definitely can," answered Emma, pressing her lips together and giving Molly a challenging, almost flirtatious look that made Molly's insides turn backflips.

"Well, thank goodness for that," said Molly, withdrawing her hand. She turned up her latte glass and downed the last drop.

CHAPTER 24
Not Like Me

Zora Neale Hurston, Tell My Horse: Voodoo & Life in Haiti & Jamaica, *1938, red and blue striped cloth cover with gilt on spine, photographs throughout. Dust jacket with colorful illustration. Hurston's studies in voodoo in Haiti and Jamaica as an anthropologist.*

Emma sat on her porch sipping tea at seven a.m. after her yoga stretches. Thinking about her last conversation with Molly, she felt that this murder investigation wasn't like her. It felt murky, and Emma didn't like to feel murky about things. Why was Molly so obsessive about this manuscript anyway? She was definitely monomaniacal about books and ephemera. *She expects me to have the same wild passion as she does for finding the manuscript and the killer of this person who seemed to have a problem with keeping his hands off books that didn't belong to him.*

The stillness was broken by a bird call. Emma heard a car motor start up a few houses down. Her neighbor across the street slammed a door, and she heard her voice calling, followed by a child's wail. Time for little Josh to go to preschool.

Emma liked Molly. She was a breath of something

new, fresh, and exciting. Her take on things was so uncomplicated. Yet she was the very opposite of simple—she had layers. Emma expected that Molly had dark places too, like everyone. She didn't seem to have a hidden agenda—except she looked at Emma a little too long and smiled a little too suggestively sometimes.

But Emma wasn't interested in a romantic relationship right now. She wasn't about to be swept away again by someone else's enthusiasms.

How passionate Gwen had been about things. Photography, rock climbing. Always looking for an outlet for her prodigious energies. But no focus. So all enthusiasms eventually fizzled. And Emma at first followed along, drawn by that force, finally learning that she could not live a life fueled by someone else's energies.

Now she led a life guided by what she cared about. Community, yes. She was no hermit. For example, she needed to email Connie about the book group's choice for next month. She wanted to read a well-written literary novel with strong, interesting characters. No more inspirational chick lit romances (wife leaves boring marriage and finds renewal through an affair) or Southern dysfunctional family sagas. She'd had enough after *The Seagrass Trail* and *Big Mama Beats Up Everybody*. Becky would suggest a rousing diatribe against capitalism, and Rachel would want to read a self-help book.

She looked around her with satisfaction. Peace and quiet, finally. Her own house, where she could do what she liked, put things where she wanted them, sleep and wake when she chose (when she could get to sleep), and read and eat and drink whatever, and whenever, she wanted. Retired from running a writing lab at a two-year college, she lived on a small pension, supplemented by savings and income from occasional freelance editing. Not the dazzling academic career she had dreamed of, but it suited the person she really was. Bookselling had not yet started to pay for itself, but it was an absorbing interest where she learned something new every day. She held her carefully balanced life in the palm of her hand, and she would not let a new person break it.

Emma drank the rest of her tea and got up. Time to meet the day. Eat a bite, do a few chores, then go to the article she was editing. She looked with satisfaction over her yard with the roses, four o'clocks, butterfly bush, and the huge, sprawling, overbearing lantana. The sun had just reached the street, and it shot a ray right into the center of Emma's garden. Pleased, she went into the house.

As she settled down at her computer, ready to pull up the article, her eyes fell on the photocopy of the note. *Whosoever readeth this boke without leave of the Circle, let him BEWARE. SF.* She was jolted when the phone rang. Despite her earlier thoughts, she hoped it might be Molly.

"Hi, Molly."

"Emma, have you heard from the police?"

"No. But I was outside for a while. I haven't checked my messages." Emma looked down at the picture of an old-time receiver with the number 2 on it. "Oh, I see I have two messages."

"They want me to come to the station. For follow-up questions. I don't know what to do. What if someone saw us go in the tunnel?"

"Tell the truth. That's the easiest way not to mix your story up."

"I'm not ready to turn over the note. Emma, promise me you won't say anything about the note or the tunnel, or that we broke in."

"If they call me, I'll just answer their questions. I doubt they'll ask if we took anything."

"Please promise me," Molly said. "We have to tell the same story."

"Okay, I promise. Let me check my messages."

"Bye, Emma."

Emma listened to her first message and heard Detective DuBois tersely ask her to call. *Maybe I am a suspect*, she thought.

CHAPTER 25
Lies and Promises

Ewen C. L'Estrange, Witch Hunting and Witch Trials, *1929, green cover with gilt on spine. Frontispiece picture of "a witch and her imps. A. D. 1621." A history of witchcraft and methods of interrogation and punishment.*

The first thing Emma noticed about Detective DuBois was her blue eyes, friendly yet sharp. The second thing was her square, jutting chin with a thin smile above it.

Emma was sitting in the detective's office in a straight-backed chair, and the detective sat across from her behind an old metal desk. It was the second time this week she had found herself facing someone behind a desk. The detective seemed more friendly than the professor. The desk creaked as the detective leaned forward, one elbow on the worn green blotter. A framed photo of a line of youngish police officers stood on the credenza behind the desk. Emma squinted and picked out the only woman, unsmiling and standing erect. It had to be DuBois.

"It must have been a shock for you, finding Mr. Hubbell's body." DuBois's manner was warm, even respectful, yet firm. Playing the good cop. Emma told herself she had nothing to hide. Nothing, that is, except that her friend took a piece of paper that might be evidence and refused to tell the police about it. Nothing except that she and said friend broke into the Booth house and rifled through the books and walked all around the floor messing up possible footprints. Emma felt her heart sink. She hated to lie—well, she hated to lie about something she wasn't sure she ought to be lying about. No, what she hated was telling someone else's lie. And she hated breaking promises. What was the worse offense, she wondered: lying to the police or breaking a promise to Molly?

"It sure was," Emma answered.

"What led you to open the door to the basement?" The detective's voice was casual, matter-of-fact.

"I heard a sound. Sounds. Voices that sounded like arguing, then a person going "Uhhh" and something heavy falling. The door was not completely closed, so I pulled it open and called out, I think, 'Is anything wrong?'"

"Did you hear anything more?"

"No—no, wait. I heard what sounded like hurried footsteps."

"Did it sound like more than one person?"

Emma tried to remember. "I don't know."

"So what made you go down into the basement? Why didn't you call someone right then?"

"I—" Emma realized she had no good reason. "I don't know. Curiosity, I suppose. And—I was worried that someone might be hurt and need help." She tried to sound candid.

DuBois looked at her with a calm expression. "So you went down out of curiosity. What did you see?"

"The first thing I saw was the bookcase, the built-in wall of bookshelves. That was level with my eyes, so it's what I noticed first." She felt defensive. Would the detective think she was callously indifferent to human life to notice the bookcase first, not the person lying on the floor? Should she mention the moving bookcase? Then the detective would ask why she hadn't mentioned it before. And why was DuBois asking her the same questions she had asked the day of the murder?

DuBois nodded. "What did you notice next?"

"I looked down and saw someone lying on the floor with books scattered all around him."

"Did you know who he was?"

"It took a second, and then I realized that it was Buck Hubbell. He tried to cut in line in front of me, and I recognized his jacket."

"Did you see anyone else?"

"No." Emma shook her head. She felt a bit of pain where the barrette she was wearing had a strand of hair in its clasp.

"But earlier, you heard footsteps."

"That's right," Emma said. "I did, when I was upstairs. But not after I was downstairs."

"Ms. Clarke, do you know of any way out of the basement other than the stairs you came down?"

Emma paused. "I'd never been in the Booth house before. I didn't even know there was a basement until I heard the sounds and went down." That wasn't a lie.

Detective DuBois looked at her a moment, eyes narrowing. "You didn't know whether there was another way into the basement?"

"No," Emma said. That was the truth—she didn't know about the tunnel then. She decided to come clean. "This will sound weird, but I thought I saw the bookcase move."

The detective's eyes opened wider. "The bookcase moved?"

"I didn't say so when you first interviewed me. I was afraid I'd imagined it."

"Why don't you think that now?"

Uh-oh, Emma thought. *Because Molly and I moved it?* "I thought I'd better tell you what I thought I saw. One part of it moved, I think."

DuBois wrote some notes and after a moment of silence, she said, "It's best to tell us as soon as you realize that there was something you omitted earlier. Now, you knew Mr. Hubbell?"

"I knew who he was, but we had never met. I've seen him at book sales. When he went to look in a window, the dealer in front of me said he was a book thief."

"A book thief?"

"That's what she said."

"And who said this?"

"Ah, Molly O'Donnell." Emma cringed inside. *Why did I have to mention Molly?* But she could not have seen a way of avoiding it.

"The person you spoke to before you called the police?"

"Yes. We had just met. I saw her in the hall when I went back up the stairs after seeing Buck—his body."

"Do you know anyone who would have reason to kill Mr. Hubbell?"

"No."

"All right, Ms. Clarke. Please stay available, as we might need to ask you a few more questions," said Detective DuBois. "And if you remember anything more, anything at all, give me a call." She smiled and stood, handing Emma a business card. As Emma took the card, the detective held onto it for half a second, her narrow eyes smiling. She let go and stepped back.

"I will," Emma said, and escaped.

CHAPTER 26
Interrogation

Edward Gall, Mysticism Throughout the Ages, *no date, brown cloth boards, black print on spine. History of mystic tradition in major religions.*

Molly couldn't sleep. As she rolled from one side of the bed to the other, her mind kept coming up with questions. What would Detective Richards ask her tomorrow? He had told her to come in first thing in the morning. She'd seen enough TV dramas to know that she'd be in a room with a one-way window so the other detectives could watch her every move, every eye twitch, every sweat gland working overtime. Had the police found her fingerprints? Had someone seen her and Emma leaving the night they broke into the Booth house basement? All her questions circled around endlessly.

She'd set her alarm for 6:20, figuring that "first thing in the morning" meant eight a.m. She allowed time for a substantial breakfast because she might be there all day, and just a half pint of yogurt wouldn't do it. Twice she'd had a dream that she woke at eleven a.m. or one p.m. and she hadn't gone to the police station. When her alarm played the opening bars of "Dream a Little

Dream of Me," she hit the snooze out of habit. But after a minute, she pulled herself out of bed. Dmitri and Blavatsky were still asleep but woke instantly when her feet hit the floor. Blavatsky barked, while Dmitri snorted and stretched. She opened their crates—"How're my good little dogs this morning?"—and out they ran towards the dog door in the back. She heard them clatter down the steps and then bark as they ran along the fence bordering the alley.

After her yogurt, supplemented by toast, half a cantaloupe, and not too much Oolong tea (not wanting to have to make a dash for the restroom in the middle of being questioned), Molly drove to the police station with plenty of time for traffic or parking difficulties. When she asked for Officer Richards, the policewoman on duty said, "He hasn't arrived yet. May I have your name?"

After Molly gave her name and why she was there, the officer said, "Oh, yes. Detective Richards said you'd be in sometime today. He was called to a homicide scene this morning. Take a seat, and someone will be with you."

Sometime today? She had a restless night when she could have strolled in whenever it suited her? Fuming, Molly sat in a straight chair and stretched out her legs.

But as usual, she had a book with her. She opened it and tried to get absorbed. But she found herself reading the same paragraph over and over again. She closed her eyes for a minute or two or more.

"Ms. O'Donnell?"

Molly jerked her head up, then up higher and recognized the tall man in a navy blue suit standing in front of her.

"Detective Richards." He held out his hand.

She stood to shake it, forcing herself alert.

The detective had a couple of file folders under his arm. "Come with me," he said, gesturing for her to follow him.

As they walked down the hall, Molly realized she was grinding her teeth. When she let her jaw go slack, her hands, which had been fists, relaxed, too. And where was Detective DuBois? Weren't she and Detective Richards both in charge of this case?

Richards opened the door to a plain-looking office. Unlike her fantasies based on numerous police dramas like *Law and Order* or *Rizzoli and Isles*, she was not entering a room with only a table and two chairs, but instead, an office with a desk and chair, photos of children at different ages, and one of Richards with two kids on a sailboat. He motioned for her to sit down across from him. She looked around for the one-way window, but the only window overlooked Peachtree Street.

"Ms. O'Donnell, when you went to the estate sale, you went into the basement, although it was clearly marked as off limits."

Oh no. She was a suspect. She tried to remember what she'd planned to say to this question, but nothing came to mind.

After what seemed a long silence, Richards said, "Hmmm?"

"I'm sorry. What was the question?" She wasn't awake enough yet for this.

"Tell me again why you went with Ms. Clarke to look at a body without calling the police first."

"She urged me to come downstairs. I think she said someone might be dead. When I first went down I checked his pulse. Then we called 911."

He leaned forward. "How well do you know Ms. Clarke?"

"We just met that day. Well, briefly in Florida last April."

"Have you talked since the day of the murder?"

"Yes."

"About the death of Mr. Hubbell?"

"Yes." She started to say that all the book dealers were talking about it, but that would bring more questions.

"Did you know Mr. Hubbell?"

"Mostly I just knew him by reputation. Occasionally we've talked at book sales."

"What do you mean, by reputation?"

"People talked about him being a book thief." Molly wondered whether she should have given out that information. But if she didn't, some other book dealer would.

"Has he stolen from you?"

"Not that I know of."

"Do you know of anyone he's stolen from?"

"I know of at least two bookstores."

He asked for names, and she reluctantly gave them.

When she finished talking, there was another awkward silence. A pencil loosely wobbled between Richards's long index finger and his thumb like a single chopstick. Letting his middle finger do the work, he tapped the eraser end against his front teeth. Was this damned tapping supposed to break her? Molly was determined to make him speak next.

"When you went into the basement, did you see anyone else?"

"No, just Emma—and Buck's body. Then Joyce came to the door, and we asked her to call the police, but I ended up doing it."

"Did you think there was someone else in the basement?"

"It did cross my mind." She clasped her hands together, almost in a prayer position, but she realized how they looked and loosened them.

"If there was someone there, how did they get out?"

She felt a wild impulse to retort, *how the heck would I know?* but restrained herself. "I don't know."

"Is there another way into and out of the basement?" (tap, tap)

"Another way?" She hoped she didn't blush. This was the point where she continued her lie and faced charges of giving false information to the police, or told the truth and admitted to breaking and entering. Giving false information couldn't possibly be as serious as breaking in. But she and Emma had entered. This guy was probably a genius at telling if people were lying by reading body language.

"You don't know?" Richards put the pencil down. "Did you think someone might be hiding in the basement or had run back up the stairs?"

She dropped her hands to her lap. It was her turn to be silent. Better not think too long or he would know she was thinking up lies. "No one could have run up the stairs because we were standing right in front of them." She licked her lips. "At one point, I did think the killer might be hiding down there."

Richards asked, "Did you hear anything when you were in the basement?"

"I don't remember. Emma and I were talking, and I was looking at a dead body. I wasn't paying much attention." She drew herself up. "I went to that estate sale to buy, and when I'm somewhere to buy books, I get pretty focused on finding them before . . ." She paused, aware she was talking too much.

Richards said, "Before?" His telephone rang. He frowned and looked at the screen. "Excuse me, I have to take this call." Speaking into his phone, he said, "Hello, Detective. Just a moment."

He wagged his fingers at Molly. "Want to step outside? You can ask Alicia to fetch you a cup of coffee."

Behind the desk in the outer office sat a plump African American woman, with very short hair, who was rubbing her upper arm with her index finger. Molly nodded to her and sat in a metal folding chair. No way was she going to ask her to fetch some coffee. Something in the office's smell reminded her of the beach.

"Oh, sorry," Alicia said to Molly. "I know I shouldn't be doing this in the office, but I thought you would be in there for a while." A tattoo script ran down the length of her glistening upper arm.

"New tat?" Molly asked to be sociable. She was interested in tattoos, but had never quite got up the nerve to get one.

"Yes," said Alicia. "My grandmother passed away last week. It's her name and dates of birth and death."

Molly leaned closer and read, "'Sadie J. Winthrop 9/23/1928~7/16/2018.' I'm sorry for your loss."

"Thank you. She had a good long life." Alicia fanned the tattooed arm.

"Still hurt?"

"A little. Rubbing it with cocoa butter feels good."

"I'd like a tattoo, but I'm afraid of the pain."

"It's more annoying than painful. I have four, so I know what to expect." Alicia showed her the inner side of her lower arm where "curiouser and curiouser" was written in script.

"Alice in Wonderland." Molly smiled, thinking of her Moser illustrated copy. She was happy to have this conversation instead of obsessing over Richards's questions.

Alicia slipped her mule off one foot to show a heart on top of her instep. "My first one. I know hearts are clichés, but what can I say? I was young and in love. Thank goodness I didn't have Frank's name or initials inside like I planned." She placed her hand over her own heart and gave a roguish smile. "I can't show you the other one, but it's an astrology symbol for Libra."

The door opened and Richards looked out. Before Alicia could get her shoe back on, he said, "Ms. O'Donnell, you are free to go. Planning any trips out of town in the near future?"

"Not until Thanksgiving. Well, sometimes I travel for auctions and, ah, estate sales."

"We may call you again, so let us know if something comes up or you remember anything about the case."

"Yes, sir, I will." Molly could really use a cup of coffee. She wondered if Emma would meet her at Oxygen. Just as he was about to shut the door, she asked, "Am I a suspect?"

"Should you be?" Without waiting for an answer, he closed the door.

CHAPTER 27
Sharing a Tart

Rudolf Steiner, The Occult Movement in the Nineteenth Century And its Relationship to Modern Culture, *1973, maroon cloth with gilt on spine. Ten lectures given in 1915 about various occult and spiritual subjects.*

Emma hunched over the tiny wrought-iron table on Oxygen's deck, staring thoughtfully into her teacup. The Earl Grey was so dark she couldn't see the bottom. "So both detectives asked us repeatedly about another entrance to the basement. And we both lied."

Molly took a long swallow of her carmelatto and set down the mug. She nodded. "So I guess we're in deeper than we thought, huh?"

"You might say that." Emma shook her head. "Lying to the police. And what happens when they find out about us breaking and entering?"

"Are they going to find out?"

"Oh, Molly. Someone may have seen us that night. One of the neighbors maybe. They might find our shoe marks, our fingerprints. You wiped them off the front door, but we left plenty on the books, all over the basement." Emma shook her head. "We're going to be found out sooner or later. Oh, why did I get mixed up in this?"

Molly said, "Maybe we ought to throw away our shoes we were wearing that day."

"I will not!" Emma said. "They're my favorites." She looked into the cup. "And now I might be a suspect. Why else would they ask you so much about me?"

Molly said, "You did go into a marked-off space first."

"Molly! Don't try to put this off onto me. It was your idea not to tell them."

"No, no, Emma. I'm not trying to do that." Molly leaned across the table. A wave of graying light brown hair fell across Molly's forehead. Her smooth skin had a few lines in the corners of her mouth and eyes. Her cheeks evidenced a permanent ruddiness that spoke of young years spent outdoors. Her blue eyes narrowed slightly, earnest, persuading. "Listen, Emma, yes, you might be their main suspect—as far as we know—but there are bound to be others. I told them Buck was well known as a book thief. They're probably calling other booksellers right now."

Emma nodded and took a sip of lukewarm tea. "I'm just worried."

The nut tart they were sharing arrived, with two napkins and two forks. The young, tattooed server smiled and said, "Anything else, ladies?" Emma noticed that Molly's eyes lingered on the tattoo, a long, twining ivy strand that wrapped around the server's lower arm and encircled her bare, toned bicep. She wondered whether Molly was attracted to younger women with tattoos.

With her fork, Emma started to halve the tart. It resisted, and she began to poke it along a line in the middle, causing the nuts to loosen and the pastry to flake.

She poked harder. The tart thunked apart, crumbs flying. Emma gave Molly the bigger half. "Why is it whenever you order tea or coffee and something sweet, your drink gets cold before the food arrives?"

Molly stood up. "I'll get you another Earl Grey," she said.

Emma shook her head. "By the time it gets here we will have finished the tart." She remembered to be polite. "I appreciate the offer though. Molly, I know you're not trying to get me into trouble. It's just that nothing like this has ever happened to me before."

Molly sat again and crossed those long, denimed legs. "So you haven't ever broken the law?"

"No," Emma said, concentrating on the tart. She began to eat her half with the fork.

"Never?"

"Well, not since grad school. That's the last time I smoked pot."

Molly kept looking at her for a few seconds longer, and Emma felt her face grow warm. Finally Molly released her gaze and turned her attention to the tart. "Mmmm. I love these. Pecans and hazelnuts with caramel." She filled her mouth with a bite and closed her eyes. She put down her fork.

As Molly pushed her plate away, Emma's eyes lingered on the last bite of tart left on it. Molly saw the glance and said, "Would you like that bite?"

"Yes, please," Emma answered. She reached with her fingers and took the morsel. It was meltingly sweet. Emma suddenly had a thought. "What about Michael? We pooh-poohed the idea, but what if he knew what was down there and when he saw Buck . . ."

"I hope Michael is on DuBois's list." Molly grimaced. "I hate for Jay and Harry to be right."

CHAPTER 28
Emma Buys Back a Stolen Book

Theodore Flournoy, From India to Planet Mars: A Study of a Case of Somnambulism, *1900, green cloth with gilt on cover and spine. About Mme. Helene Smith (pseudonym of a French medium), who channels spirits and also habitants of Mars. Large section on Mars and its language and botany.*

"Hello?" Emma put her phone to her ear with one hand while holding the pruners in her right. Being a southpaw, she had trouble getting her fingers in the right places.

"Hello, Emma? This is Fred."

"Oh, hi, Fred." She cast about in her memory for a Fred.

"Fred Bailey, we met at the ABOG meeting. How're you doing?"

"Fine," she answered by rote. Oh, yes, he was the white-bearded guy who was the president of ABOG. Her memory opened up further, showing her the vast room for books that he had added on to his house. The room where—uh-oh—she had found the C.S. Lewis book. And had taken it. She walked to the porch and laid the pruners on the railing.

"Um, Emma, I received a package in the mail today, a book. It's a book I already have, a C.S. Lewis. I was wondering why you sent it to me. I don't have any record of buying it from you. I wouldn't anyway, since I have one and don't want another right now. Can't sell that one."

Oh, why did she put her return address on the box? "Ah, Fred, I have something to tell you—that's your book." She tried to think fast of something that would make sense. Nothing came. She ploughed desperately onward: "I—was looking at it that day of the meeting, and—something distracted me—and when I got home, I found it was in my bag. I must have slipped it in without being aware." She shrank inside. She would not have believed this story herself.

"So it's my book?" Fred's voice sounded incredulous. He gave a gruff laugh. "Well, okay. Glad to get it back. Sure you don't want to buy it? I'll give you a good price. How about thirty percent off?"

Emma felt a surge of excitement. Why hadn't she thought of asking Fred if she could buy it in the first place? She could actually own the book. "As a matter of fact, I would like to buy it."

"Great." He named a price. "And I've got some Narnia books you might like."

"Sure, I'll take a look at them." She was feeling expansive. And guilty.

After making plans to go to Fred's to pick up *Against the Diabolical*, she hung up. "Wow!" she breathed. She was going to make it right and buy the book. No more Emma the Book Thief, although that would definitely be better than Emma the Murderer.

☙☙☙

She arrived at Fred's house at three o'clock. As she went up the brick walkway, she sniffed with appreciation the wormwood, rue, rosemary, and other herbs that tangled around the narrow path. Before she reached the brick stoop, the door burst open and a woman charged out. She was tall, blonde, and wearing high heels. It was Dr. Shirley Parnell.

"Hi," Emma said, stepping aside to avoid being pushed into the shrubbery.

Dr. Parnell turned her head, breaking her fierce trajectory. Her eyes widened with surprise. She glared as though she wanted to blast Emma out of existence.

Emma shrank back. She started to speak, but before she could get a word out, Dr. Parnell dashed away down the path, jumped into a blue, late-model Audi parked on the curb, and roared away.

Puzzled, Emma went up to the door and knocked. Sarah answered, looking not like her usual cheerful self. Her round, pretty face looked tighter and older. Her mouth was set in a straight line, and her eyes narrowed suspiciously. She was wearing a long patchwork skirt and a denim vest over a flowing white top.

"Yes?" she said.

"Hi, Sarah," Emma said. "I'm here to see Fred about a book."

Sarah still stared at her with a look of suspicion and something else that Emma couldn't quite place. Then Sarah seemed to remember where she was, and her face cleared a little. But the unaccustomed lines around the tight mouth stayed. "Oh, yes. Hi, Emma. Sorry, come on in."

Emma wanted to ask if everything was okay, but something forbade her. There was too much tension around Sarah.

"Go on into the book annex," said Sarah. "He's expecting you."

Emma felt a little creeping chill around the back of her neck, for no reason she could explain.

But then Fred, looking bearish, smiled as she entered the book annex. His beard was braided in a long tapering plait. "Hi, Emma. I've got your book right here. Sure you don't want the set of Narnia?"

"Mmmm, I don't know if I can make a profit on it."

"I can give you thirty percent off the set, too."

"Let me think about it. I saw it the other day." She felt she owed it to him, since he was being so genial about the book she lifted. "Sure. I'll take it."

"It's a beautiful set." He conveniently had it sitting on his worktable. He slipped *Against the Diabolical* out of the box she had mailed it in and put it on top of the Narnias. While he waited for his tablet to power up, he grumbled about how you couldn't sell good books like this anymore, there wasn't a market. Emma was half listening and half wondering what Dr. Parnell had been doing there. Did she buy the other books she wrote about in her dissertation, such as the *Space Trilogy*, from him? Emma's eyes drifted to the shelves above her. A sky-blue dust wrapper with scroll gold lettering caught her attention. It was in a box with two other books. She went over and took a closer look. *Perelandra*, by C.S. Lewis. It was the second in Lewis's *Space Trilogy*.

She had read the *Space Trilogy* years ago when she was into science fiction. It started out with a space travel story and led into a battle of good versus evil just as in the Narnia books, with the forces of good clearly Christian, with a strong Renaissance flavor, and the forces of evil as clearly diabolical black magic.

She took hold of the blue-jacketed book and tried to pull it out of the box. It was between the other two books and was wedged rather tightly. She worked it gently, and it came out. She opened it and carefully pulled off the dust jacket to look at the boards. The book looked to be in near fine condition. No marks, only a little rubbing on the spine. The inside showed only a little tanning with age. She replaced the jacket and pushed the book back between its two mates. "By the way, how much would you take for the *Space Trilogy*?" she asked.

Fred quoted her a price.

"I'll take it, also." She really ought to examine the other two books, but it had been hard enough getting one out of the box. She decided to assume they were equally fine. Fred had a sterling reputation as a dealer—she trusted him.

After sliding her debit card through his reader (the card still worked, thank goodness), and signing with her finger, she said, "Fred, was that Dr. Parnell leaving your house?"

"Dr.?" He looked quizzical and said, "That woman? Uh, she's a friend, or acquaintance maybe, of Sarah's." He stood and handed her the bag of books. Chuckling, he added, "This is one of my strangest sales, but I'm not complaining."

As she walked down the path toward her car, the rue and wormwood brushing against her ankles, she realized what emotion had been on Sarah's face besides suspicion. It was fear.

CHAPTER 29
Dr. Parnell Tells a Tale

Thomson Hudson, The Law of Psychic Phenomena: A Working Hypothesis and the Systematic Study of Hypnotism, Spiritism, Mental Therapeutics, Etc., *1893, blue cloth with gilt on spine. Relationship of psychic experiences including mesmerism, hypnotism, somnambulism, trance, spiritism, demonology, and miracles.*

Emma was sitting at Molly's dining room/work table putting Mylar on dust jackets for the next book fair when her phone rang. When she heard Dr. Parnell's voice, she sat up straight.

"I'm afraid I was a bit rude when you were in my office the other day," said the professor, "and I'd like to apologize. Also, I'd like to talk with you more about the book you mentioned. Would you have dinner with me tonight? My treat. I'd like to invite you to Sophia's. It's a really nice Turkish restaurant in Decatur. Some friends of mine run it."

Surprised, Emma agreed. As she ended the call, she said, "Well, that was weird. Have you ever been to that Turkish restaurant, Sophia's, in Decatur?"

"No," Molly said. "I've heard it's pretty good."

"I'm going there tonight, as it happens." Emma

peered at the Yelp reviews on her phone. "With Dr. Shirley Parnell, no less."

"What?" Molly sat up straight. "I didn't know you were so friendly with her."

"I'm not. She just called me, out of the blue, and invited me to have dinner at Sophia's. She said she wanted to talk more about that book I mentioned, the one C.S. Lewis wrote about." Emma turned her phone off. "The kebabs and cucumber salad got good reviews. At least I'll get a tasty dinner."

"Wow!" Molly said. "She's inviting you to talk about *A Boke of Secret Knowlege*. I knew she had it, or knows where it is."

"I think you're right. But why ask me to dinner?"

Molly shrugged. "Maybe she wants to make up for being so rude before."

Emma frowned. "Maybe. But I don't get it." She pulled thoughtfully at one of Blavatsky's soft ears and got a lick on her fingers in response.

Molly leaned forward eagerly. "What an opportunity! I wish I could go."

"I'm meeting her at 7:00," Emma said. "Why don't you give me a call around 8:30? If everything's all right, I'll answer. If it's not, I won't."

"What are you worried about?"

"I don't know, but I feel nervous."

"What should I do if you don't answer?"

"Come to Sophia's and ask for us. Say we're expecting you."

Molly agreed. "You get to have the adventure," she said, mock-pouting.

"Believe me, I wish it were you instead of me."

"That's okay," Molly said. "I'll spend the evening curled up with a good book. Thanks for lending me *The*

Space Trilogy. I'm looking forward to it."

Loud thumps sounded as Blavatsky began to scratch vigorously. Molly glanced at the dog. "She's just had her flea treatment, so she shouldn't be itching. She picks up on my worry sometimes."

※ ※ ※

Emma easily located Sophia's using her phone map. She parked in the gravel lot behind the restaurant and walked around to the front door, where Shirley Parnell stood waiting, her pale blonde hair framing her face. She looked rather melancholy, thought Emma. The professor smiled when she saw Emma, a quick, elastic smile. "Did you have any trouble finding the place, Dr. Clarke?"

"Please call me Emma."

"Shirley."

They shook hands.

Inside the small, dimly lit restaurant, a dark-haired woman came out from behind a counter to greet Shirley with a hug and lead them to a quiet table in a corner. Emma looked with approval at the tent created by draperies on the ceiling. The kebabs were perfectly grilled with rosemary, the saffron pilaf fluffy, the cucumbers crisp, dressed with a lemony vinaigrette and tossed with ripe cherry tomatoes, Kalamata olives, and spring onions.

As they ate, they talked about the restaurant, owned by friends of Shirley's, and how good the food was. Shirley led the talk to books and writers of the Renaissance. Soon Emma found herself discussing Paracelsus, Giordano Bruno, and John Dee. Shirley was a charming and erudite conversationalist well versed in scholarship on alchemy and occult philosophy. Emma decided she rather liked her.

"Alchemists weren't trying to make gold," the professor said. "They were seeking union with—transcendence."

"Dame Frances Yates says they were seeking God," Emma said.

Shirley's face tightened.

The main course was followed by honey-soaked baklava and concluded with tiny glasses of liqueur that burned Emma's throat. Once past the burn, she luxuriated in the warm, thick sensation that radiated from her belly to her chest. "Simon Forman mentions summoning angels and demons," she said, going back to the astrologer, "but he doesn't seem to feel that he's doing anything evil."

Shirley looked directly at Emma. "Forman was an interesting character, wasn't he?"

"Yes," Emma said. "He's very—"

Shirley interrupted. "Would you like to smoke a hookah? They have nice rooms in the back, and water pipes, and really good Turkish tobacco."

Emma, surprised, said, "I don't want to smoke, but I'll be glad to go and sit with you."

Shirley told the waiter they would like to smoke some argila. He led them through a beaded curtain to a small room. Draperies covered the walls and hung over the light fixtures, creating a dim glow that made it hard for Emma to see the table. They were served tiny cups of thick, sweet coffee and presented with an impressive brass hookah, decorated with intricate carvings of leaves and vines. The design curved around the hookah in sharp black relief. Emma thought she saw a snake among the vines, but it was only another vine. Two hoses were draped around the stem.

Emma said, continuing the conversation, "So didn't Simon Forman leave a lot of unpublished manuscripts?"

Shirley lit the scented tobacco and lifted one of the mouthpieces of the hookah to her lips. She inhaled, held the smoke in her lungs for a moment, and released a cloud of smoke. Emma thought of Alice and the caterpillar.

"He certainly did," said Shirley. "In fact, he only published one book in his lifetime. It and his unpublished manuscripts are in the Ashmole collection in the Bodleian." She paused. "But you know that already, don't you?"

"I've studied Forman a little," Emma said. "But do you know of any of his manuscripts that aren't there?"

Shirley looked hard at Emma, her glance unreadable. "You were asking me earlier about a book that C.S. Lewis describes in *Against the Diabolical*, when he relates that tragic episode that led to the death of young Lord Agerton. Isn't that right?"

"Yes," Emma answered. "I wondered whether you had ever seen it."

"What if I were to tell you that I have seen it, that I have held it in my hands and used it?"

"*Used* it?"

Shirley gave a light chuckle, lips pressed together. "You know the book's title, of course?"

"*A Boke of Secret Knowlege by a Learned Doctor.*"

Shirley's voice was almost reverent. "What kind of 'secret knowledge' do you suppose it contains?"

Emma started to answer again, but Shirley stopped her. "You know about Bernard H. Booth, the wealthy antiquarian who died recently here in Atlanta?" Emma nodded. "And you know about the library he left at his death in the basement of his home?"

"I went to the estate sale."

"But do you know about the meetings held in his basement, meetings that had been going on long before Bernard inherited the house from his mother? Did you know, by the way, that his mother was the sister of Lord Agerton?"

"What?" Emma exclaimed.

Shirley continued, "And that she—and her son after her—were noted practitioners of Ceremonial Magic?"

Emma felt she would burst with excitement.

Shirley smiled. "So let me tell you a story." She lifted the pipe to her lips, inhaled, and blew out a cloud of scented smoke. "I met Bernard Booth when I was in graduate school at Candler. I liked him immediately. After talking, we discovered we were distant cousins. He was a wise old man, a bearded wizard with one earring. He seemed to have depths of knowledge hidden, unspoken, but his smile and his eyes seemed to convey that you were special, that you would be one of the few, the very few, whom he might trust."

Emma lifted her tiny cup of Turkish coffee and sipped the sweet, thick liquid. The odor of smoke from the hookah infused around her, mint and tobacco.

"He invited me to a small gathering," continued Shirley, "where he said some academic and professional friends would be, people who shared our interests in the Renaissance (he hated calling it 'Early Modern'), in alchemy, occult philosophy, the Cabala. I went. I was surprised by the house. I don't know, I suppose I expected it to be more picturesque, a sort of cross between the House of Seven Gables and Hogwarts." She laughed self-consciously. "But it was an ordinary ranch house like I grew up in. Later I learned that Bernard's family had an old clapboard farmhouse on that site. When it burned down, the current house was built over the existing basement."

Emma kept on her listening face and took another drink. The grounds on the bottom of the cup tasted like spiced mud.

"We met in the living room and had drinks," continued Shirley, "and I was enjoying myself. I met some long-time friends of his. His cousin sat beside him on a footstool." Shirley's voice took on a faint sneer. "He smiled at her as though she were a charming child. Later I found out she was his heir." Her mouth twisted into a frown. "He couldn't see what a little schemer she was, always trying to worm her way into power. She had him fooled for a while. That hippie-dippie act made me want to puke." She sucked on the mouthpiece and, with an audible exhale, sent a curl of smoke floating up over her head.

Emma felt a bit taken aback by Shirley's sudden hostility. She felt the urge to cough, from the secondary smoke, and suppressed it. She also felt a little wobbly from all the information, as well as from the cucumbers, baklava, coffee, and smoke.

"After a while, most of the people left, coming up to him and shaking his hand as though he were a godfather or a king. Bernard laid his hand on my wrist, signaling me to remain. Quiet fell, and Bernard looked at those of us who were left. After a moment, he nodded, and people began to get up and go toward the hall. He motioned to me and I followed him down the stairs to the basement."

Emma tensed. She breathed slowly, waiting to hear what came next.

"He turned on the light," Shirley continued, "and I gasped when I saw the books. He smiled at my astonishment. 'You can look your fill at the library, but only the initiated can go further,' he said. 'I must join the others now. You can find your way out.' He pulled a book off the shelf, and someone pushed the spring on a bookcase, and it swung outward. I watched as they all followed Bernard into a room. The door closed behind them. I felt suddenly excluded, jealous, and curious about what was going on."

Shirley paused and drew in more smoke. "Sure you won't have a puff? It's only a little bit of tobacco and mint leaves." She dangled a woven golden hose.

"No, thank you," Emma said. Excitement and sudden sleepiness warred within her. She couldn't wait to hear Shirley's story, and she also felt that she would like to sink to the floor, curl up, and go to sleep right on the Turkish carpet. The black vines on the hookah seemed to weave and twine around one another. Did the snake raise its head and hiss? She shook her head, trying to clear it.

Shirley went on, "I defended my dissertation, but my committee rejected it. I was devastated. I knew it wasn't that my dissertation wasn't good. I had done my research thoroughly. But my major advisor didn't agree with me. I suggested that Alfred Harford, Lord Agerton, had died because C.S. Lewis refused to participate in a ritual that would have saved him."

Emma frowned. "A ritual would have saved him? What ritual?"

"Alfred left Oxford at the end of the term, and his family collected all his belongings. Later in the summer, Lewis was contacted by one of Alfred's close friends. The friend said that Alfred was very 'ill of an unknown malady'—his words—and that he suspected it had something to do with a ritual that went wrong. He suggested that a being or entity was angry that Lewis had broken a closed circle and was taking vengeance on Alfred. He begged Lewis to come and participate in a ritual that, he hoped, would save Alfred by placating the being. Lewis refused."

Emma felt she had walked into a horror novel. "How do you know this?"

Shirley paused. "I saw a letter in Alfred's papers in the Harford Collection at the Bodleian. His family must have missed it. It was unsigned, no envelope, creased and re-creased. It was in a handwriting that looked like Lewis's, but I couldn't prove that it was. It read, 'You must be mad to suggest such a thing. My presence would not help, and I certainly will not participate in such trumped-up folly. I will pray for you.'"

"What became of the letter?" asked Emma.

Shirley said in a flat voice, "It disappeared. When I went back, it wasn't there. So I had no proof. I told my advisor that I had seen it, but she only pooh-poohed my claim, as well as my suggestion that a ritual might save someone's life. I continued with my dissertation, arguing that Lewis's guilt over the whole incident had an impact on the rest of his life and work. She still rejected the dissertation. She didn't want to approve anything that made Lewis look bad."

Emma wished she had read the whole dissertation instead of zeroing in on the *Boke*. Her head felt light on her neck, like one of those bobble dolls.

"I know, I know—a moral dilemma! He would look like a bad Christian if he did participate in the ritual, and he would look like a bad friend if he didn't. My advisor wanted no part of it. Most of all, she didn't want to put her signature on a paper that might suggest any student of hers was into 'that woo-woo stuff.'" Shirley sniffed. "She was Catholic. Talk about 'woo-woo'! I poured out my frustrations to Bernard, who listened and gave me bland advice about making the recommended revisions. I was getting ready to leave when Bernard stopped me. He said, 'You don't trust us yet, do you? You must trust before you can receive.' I said of course I trusted him. And he asked me if I wanted to join the Circle."

"The Circle?" Emma almost gasped at the word.

Shirley smiled. "Yes. The Circle. The Circle that Alfred, Lord Agerton, was heir to, that his sister Claire Harford Booth led after his death, and that her son Bernard led after her. The Circle that Simon Forman began in 1609, and that has been in continuous existence since that date."

Emma stared, all thought of sleep forgotten.

Shirley continued. "I had longed to know, to experience what went on behind that door. And I wanted to be closer to Bernard. So I made the decision to join. I was excited and terrified at the same time. I went through an initiation into Ceremonial Magic. A table like an altar stood at the far end with candles. We all circled around a fresh chalk pentagram that had been drawn on the floor, and Bernard took his place behind the altar. He wore a drapery like a minister's stole with embroidery on it. He took up the *Boke of Secret Knowlege*—yes, the very same *Boke*—placed it on the altar, and opened it. It is our grimoire, you see—our book of spells." Her smile grew misty, as though she were beholding a vision.

Emma thought, *So she was not forthcoming in her dissertation about where the Boke is.*

"He began to read from it, and the ceremony began. What happened transformed my life. It opened me up so deeply to Bernard and to all of them to an extent that I felt bound to them."

Emma stayed still, not wanting to break whatever spell was causing Shirley to tell her so much. She focused her mind, willing Shirley to go on.

"I began going to see Bernard more. We had so many good talks, just the two of us." Shirley sighed. "And he started giving me instructions for spells. Yes, spells. At first, minor ones for finding lost objects, that kind of thing. The materials were innocent, no more than herbs, leaves, roots, bark. I tried them, determined to never go further, that I would venture only as far in Magic as felt right to me. I wouldn't harm anyone or anything. Bernard indulged me. But there was one hitch. His spells worked for small things, but not for what I wanted."

"What did you want?" murmured Emma.

Shirley looked at her. "My doctorate, of course. And a tenure track position." She heaved an exasperated sigh. "So I submitted my dissertation again with the committee's changes, but my advisor still disagreed with my thesis and refused to sign off. I told Bernard, and he finally agreed with me that no changes I made would satisfy her. He said there was only one way to make sure my dissertation was approved, and that he could give me a spell for it." She shook her head. "I was appalled at first, but I wanted my Ph.D. so badly that I agreed. He gave me instructions, which I followed. They were—a bit off-putting." She hesitated. "Anyway, what do you think happened?" She smiled a quiet, thin smile that made Emma shiver.

Emma whispered, fearful of the answer, "What?"

"My advisor died." Shirley gazed into Emma's eyes, an unblinking stare. Her green eyes glistened like glass. "Her car ran off the road and burst into flames."

Emma gasped. Her spine had turned to ice. She lifted her cup to her lips and set it down. It held nothing but the undrinkable mud at the bottom.

After a moment, Shirley went on. "Another member of my committee became my advisor, and he agreed that I supported my thesis, and so my dissertation was approved."

"So you continued—in the Circle?"

"Yes, I did." Shirley's lips looked blurred from the hookah, but her eyes gleamed, fixed on Emma. "You understand, don't you?"

Part of Emma did understand: the part that had applied for tenure track jobs and been turned down time after time. Would she have done what Shirley did? Maybe, at a certain time in her life. She closed her eyes a moment and breathed a prayer of gratitude that such a path had not been offered to her.

Shirley continued. "I can tell you're thinking that this is crazy or evil. It isn't either. Sometimes it's benevolent. I gave people things, rewarded those who helped me. My new advisor went from Associate Professor to Full Professor and, after hiring me, is now Department Head. But, as Bernard used to say, dark and light are both sides of the same coin, and a seeker must not draw back at the gate beyond where opposites meet." Shirley gazed out into the room as though looking intently at something or someone. Emma almost looked around, and the back of her neck prickled. She realized that Shirley was a seeker, someone longing to believe in something larger than herself. Magic was her religion.

"So who became the leader of the Circle after Bernard?"

"I did," Shirley said. She took a puff and let out a stream of smoke that slowly climbed above her head. "I am his true heir. He told me so before he died."

The smoky air lay heavily aromatic, almost tactile, around them, and Emma felt her throat getting scratchy. She coughed and wished for some water. She avoided looking at the intertwining design on the pipe because there was definitely movement. Did that pipe contain just tobacco? She had never smoked opium. Could that be what it was? And *when* was Molly going to call? It was too dark to read her watch.

"Emma." Shirley's voice cut through her thoughts. "You know, it could work for you too."

"What could work for me?"

"Magic," said Shirley. "It's not for everybody, that goes without saying. Most educated people think it's pure hooey, and ordinary people believe in it and are scared to pieces. The movies and TV have convinced them of all kinds of hidden conspiracies, from space aliens in Roswell to the predictions of Nostradamus. Most of my colleagues think science explains everything—while knowing less than nothing about science—while my students and their families would gleefully burn me at the stake if they knew the half of it. And then—there are people like you."

Emma felt wary. "People like me?"

"You're highly intelligent, you go your own way, and you're open to possibilities." Shirley's green eyes seemed to glow with a light of their own. Her voice grew softer. "You're a Renaissance woman scholar, not drawn in by what lures most women: marriage, children, family." Her voice held just a touch of scorn for these. "A woman apart, who sees with clear eyes. A woman with desires not met by the ordinary, the obvious."

Emma felt warm and expansive for a moment, then annoyed. *What's she getting at?* she thought. "Why are you telling me all this?"

Shirley said in a low voice, "Because I thought you would understand. I think you respect mystery." She wrapped both hoses tight around the stem of the hookah and pushed it to the edge of the round table.

Emma nodded, almost unwilling. She hoped she wouldn't have to catch the hookah if it fell. She took a deep breath. "So what are you asking, exactly?"

Shirley kept that intent gaze fixed on her. "Are you interested?"

Emma paused. "In what?"

Shirley gave a slight laugh. "You know what I mean." She lightly touched Emma's hair, brushing it backward. Emma shivered involuntarily.

And then a narrow stream of clarity pierced the mist in her mind. Shirley had used the exact words that Emma would like to hear used about herself. *She's trying to seduce me, though not sexually. She's trying to draw me over to her side.*

Emma shook her head as though to clear it. "You don't know me," she said, looking straight into Shirley's eyes. "You don't know me at all."

Shirley looked at her with a hard gleam in her eyes. "No," she said. "I don't suppose I do." Then her tone abruptly changed. "Maybe you're right, maybe it isn't for you. Forget what I've said, forget it all. It's nothing."

Emma felt puzzled, but then a line from a play floated into her mind, and a chill came over her: *"O*

Faustus, leave these frivolous demands/ That strike a terror to my fainting soul." Marlowe's Doctor Faustus, Mephistopheles *giving the obligatory warning. Did Shirley think she was bound to give it? Was she bound to give it?*

Emma felt ice roll down her spine. She said as steadily as she could, "That's right. What you propose isn't for me."

Shirley drew back slightly. "But you know where the *Boke* is. You said you did that day you were in my office."

Surprised, Emma shook her head. "No, I didn't say that."

"You said what if it turned up in Atlanta."

Emma gave a bubble of a laugh. "But I didn't mean—I don't know where it is."

"Don't lie." Shirley's voice was too soft, too close. "I know you have it."

"*I* have it? No! You have it!"

Shirley looked patient and exasperated, as though with a slow student. "Emma, why would you have said that if you didn't know where it was?"

"I—I didn't mean anything by it!" Her stomach tightened. When *was* Molly going to call? Wasn't it eight-thirty yet?

"Then why did you say it?" Shirley's eyes bored into hers.

"It was an idle remark. You said it was lost, and I was saying, maybe it isn't, maybe it's here. But I don't know anything about it."

"Emma, I need that book. I have to have it."

"Why?"

"Because—" Shirley's voice became more exasperated. "I can't let it fall into Sarah's hands. She says she's the heir, the true leader of the Circle. Some of the other members support her. They don't believe that Bernard chose me."

"But, I don't understand," Emma said, feeling as though she were in that basement again, only this time it was locked and Shirley held the key. She began to breathe hard. Suddenly she felt a vibrating sensation that she almost didn't recognize. Her phone! She started to reach for her pocket, then stopped. Molly would get the message that something was wrong if she didn't answer. She put her hand back on the table. "If you're the true heir, surely you have proof."

"I had Bernard's word and seal." Shirley's voice ground out the words.

"Oh." Emma began to understand. "You don't have any written proof. But if you have the book—"

"Possession of *A Boke of Secret Knowlege* has been always the sign of leadership in this Circle." Shirley shook her head. "But that aging hippy, hairy-legged floozy in her droopy-drapey patchwork outfits, *she* insists that Bernard named *her* his heir because she is a Harford and his cousin. But I'm related to him, too."

A sudden flash of realization dawned on Emma. "Sarah?" she blurted out. "Not—Fred's Sarah? Sarah Bailey?"

"Yes, yes, Fred's Sarah," snapped Shirley. "Sarah Harford Bailey. Who else?"

"*That's* why you were at their house the other day! You went there to—"

"*You* went there, and she gave it to you!"

"No!" Emma said. "I went to see Fred about—"

Shirley rose from her seat. "We're going to your house. Now."

"Right now? Why?"

"No more questions. We're going to go get that book."

"But I told you I don't have it! And besides, I'm not finished with my coffee." Emma clutched the tiny cup as though it were a charm.

Shirley lifted Emma's cup and turned it upside down, spilling the grounds on the tablecloth. "Come on, let's go." She seized Emma's arm and pulled her to her feet. Emma clutched at the table to keep from falling.

As they left the restaurant, Shirley spoke to the hostess and pressed a bill in her hand while keeping tight hold onto Emma. The hostess beamed back at Shirley and, leaning over, placed a kiss on her cheek. Emma started to speak, but the woman gave her a cold stare, and Emma knew that she too was part of this.

Shirley propelled Emma toward her own car.

"My car—" protested Emma.

"Later," hissed Shirley. "Get in." She pushed Emma into the back seat and slammed the door. Emma grappled with the unlock button over and over, but it wouldn't work. There must be a child-lock on. Shirley ran around to the driver's side, flung open the door, and slid in. As she started the car with a roar, Emma briefly thought of beating on the window, screaming—she remembered with a sudden terror—*the car in the ditch, fire!*

Shirley peeled out of the parking lot like a Daytona racer.

"Do you know how to get to my house?" gasped Emma, hanging on to the seat belt. She hadn't even gotten it fastened.

"Of course I know," muttered Shirley, screeching around a corner and dodging parked cars as she plowed along a narrow Decatur street.

Emma bit her lip and hung on to the loose seat belt as they flashed through the dark.

CHAPTER 30
What Molly Found

Camille Flammarion, Uranie, *1896, green cloth with gilt stamp on front cover and gilt lettering and illustration on spine. Life after death, the universe, infinity, and life on Mars.*

Molly settled into her most comfortable chair and pushed a pillow behind her back, while another one cradled her neck. After she sipped from her cup of chamomile tea, its smell reminiscent of fresh apples, she reached for the slipcase that housed the three volumes of C. S. Lewis's *Space Trilogy*: *Out of the Silent Planet* in a red dust jacket, *Perelandra* in blue, and *That Hideous Strength* in black. She felt a pleasant sense of anticipation as she hooked her fingers over the spine of the first book: *Out of the Silent Planet*.

She had been an avid reader of science fiction in her teens and twenties, devouring Isaac Asimov, Arthur C. Clarke, Theodore Sturgeon, and Ray Bradbury. But she was put off by the machismo and stereotyped female characters. When she discovered feminist science fiction and fantasy, her joy knew no bounds: Vonda McIntyre, Joanna Russ, Marion Zimmer Bradley, Ursula K.

LeGuin. She had avoided Lewis, thinking him not a real science fiction writer. Drifting away from science fiction and fantasy, she had returned to the speculative with her interest in the occult, first to read and collect, now to sell. Now she was an omnivorous reader.

The red-jacketed book was hard to budge. Molly pulled gently, trying to get a purchase on the spine of the book but not wanting to damage it or the box. She wiggled it back and forth and finally pulled it loose from the case.

It was then she saw what had made the book fit so tightly. A thin booklet encased in a plastic bag lay wedged between *The Silent Planet* and the board of the slipcase. She pulled it out. It was stiff, browned with age. Must be some sort of ephemera related to Lewis. She ran her finger along the plastic lips and, pulling them apart, took careful hold of the booklet.

As soon as she felt it in her hands, Molly knew what it was. She felt chills run over her body. Her breath came quickly. Her quest was over and she couldn't wait to open the book.

It was thinner than she had expected it to be, and smaller. Only five by seven inches and about twenty pages thick. Small enough to fit inside a plastic sandwich bag and lie unnoticed between the wall of a slipcase and a book. But easy to find, if someone knew where to look. Did Fred know about *A Boke* being inside the slipcase? Who put it there? What did its being there mean?

She ran her fingertips over the brittle cover. Foxed, stained, and edged with small tears, the little volume looked to be hand-stitched. Molly's heart thudded as she read the faded inscription in a large Jacobean secretary hand: *A Boke of Secret Knowlege by A Learned*

Doctor.

Molly cautiously lifted the cover. The inside pages were of delicate, time-stained paper, covered with small handwriting and diagrams. A bit of brown paper fell off as she tried to turn the first page with a careful hand, and she caught it and put it back between the pages. On a page about halfway through, she saw a detailed engraving of a demon's face—smushed pug nose as though pressed against glass, long, pointed tusks curving up from the lower jaw over swollen cheeks, baleful eyes glaring out at her. The edge of the page was lighter than the middle, as though a smaller piece of paper or something had lain over the demon's face. The warning note! She had to fit the note over the page. Standing, she noticed the mantel clock. The time was eight-forty-two. Emma! She was supposed to call Emma at eight-thirty. Pulling her phone out of her pocket, she dialed and listened to Emma's phone ring once, twice, three times. Then she heard Emma's recorded voice.

She dialed again, and once more it went to voice mail. She felt annoyed, but then remembered Emma saying, "If everything is all right, I'll answer. If it isn't, I won't."

Molly sprang toward the door and was almost out when she looked back at the little manuscript lying on the arm of her chair. Quickly she picked it up and slid it back into its protective baggie. She started to put it back into the *Space Trilogy* slipcase. But no, that was where it would be expected to be. She looked around and finally lifted half a stack of magazines on her coffee table and placed the plastic-wrapped booklet—the *Boke*—among them. She shoved *Out of the Silent Planet* back into the case, set the case under a stack of other books, and dashed out the door.

CHAPTER 31
The Eve of Destruction

Annie Besant, A Study in Consciousness: A Contribution to the Study of Psychology, *1904, blue cloth with art nouveau style design on front. Title in gilt on front cover and spine. A Theosophical look at human consciousness based on Hindu origins.*

Shirley Parnell brought the Audi to a shuddering halt in Emma's driveway. "Go inside, I'm right behind you."
Emma heard a click—the car door was unlocked. She pushed it open. She struggled to stand. Why was she so woozy? Could fear do that? No, that coffee must have been drugged.

Rain had been falling. Under the porch light, Emma saw muddy footprints on the brick walkway that led from the front walk around the corner of the house. She stopped. "Someone's been here."

"Go on, open the door," said Shirley through clenched teeth.

Emma glanced at the holly bushes that bristled out over the brick walkway. A few branches had been broken off, as though someone bulky had pushed past them. A sheaf of swamp daisies that fell over the walkway had been trampled.

Emma's hand trembled so much she could hardly fit her key into the front doorlock. The light was on. "Someone's here!" she said. "I'm not going in."

"Go on!" Shirley gave her a shove, and Emma stumbled through the door. She wasn't only sleepy, she was clumsy, too.

Almost rigid with fear, Emma looked around her living room and gave an involuntary cry. The room had been wrecked. Chairs turned over, cushions slashed, lamps smashed, books flung around over everything, pages torn, even the covers of some ripped off.

Emma covered her eyes with her hands as she heard Shirley suck in a breath. Emma got the nerve to uncover her eyes and call out, "Who's there?"

No sound. Heavy silence. Holding onto a chair, she stood motionless. Shirley was behind her, between her and the door, making no sound. Emma went cautiously forward, stepping around the pile of books, sofa cushions, and overturned end tables. She went into her study where she saw the same kind of destruction. More books thrown about and ripped up. She moved like a sleepwalker around the room, touching the top of the desk, the leg of the overturned chair, a book flattened on the desktop.

She tapped on her bedroom door before pushing it open. The room was untouched. Whoever had done this either had decided it wasn't worth their time to rampage through the bedroom or had to leave fast.

She sank down on the bed, looking up in a daze at Shirley Parnell standing in the doorway. Shirley stared, pale and slack-mouthed, then her eyes widened. "Sarah!" she hissed as she turned and ran out the front door.

Emma heard Shirley's car roar out of the driveway.

She sat absently playing with the chenille coverlet on the bed, then she realized she had to call the police. After reporting the burglary, she slowly realized that someone was pounding on the front door. "Go away!" she shouted.

"Emma! Are you in there?" It was Molly's voice.

"Molly!" Emma ran to the door, bypassing the piles of debris on the floor. She seized Molly's hands and pulled her into the house.

"I went to the restaurant," Molly said, breathing hard. "The hostess looked at me blankly when I asked about you, but—" She stopped talking as her eyes took in the living room. "Oh, my god," she whispered, looking around, eyes wide. She turned back to Emma. "Are you okay?"

"Yeah, I think so," Emma said, surprised at how normal her voice sounded to herself. "But look at my living room."

"What happened?" asked Molly, looking around. "And—wait—where's your car?"

Emma blew out a whooshing breath. "Where to start? Let's go outside." The cool night air was refreshing after that smoky restaurant. They both sat in rocking chairs on Emma's porch, and Emma began to recount the evening to Molly. She had just gotten to Shirley saying, "We're going to your house," when a police car drove up and two uniformed officers got out.

"Ms. Clarke?" one asked.

"Yes," Emma said, standing.

The shorter officer looked around the house while Emma talked to the taller one, who filled out a report of the crime.

"Think you'll find them?" asked Emma, without much hope.

"Not unless they try to sell or pawn something, and you can identify it. Do you have the serial numbers of anything they took?" asked the tall officer.

Emma shook her head. "They tore up my house, so I don't know if they took anything. I think they were looking for something and didn't find it."

The officer raised her eyebrows. "What were they looking for?"

Emma took a deep breath. "It may have something to do with a murder investigation that Detectives DuBois and Richards are working on. The Hubbell murder."

The officer looked more alert. "Murder? We'll tell them about this. Are you staying here tonight?"

"I am," Emma said, the firmness in her voice surprising herself.

"Maybe you should have someone stay with you."

Emma hesitated.

Molly said, "I'll stay with her."

The short officer had been looking through the house. He now came back and said, "They got out through the back door. It's open. And they came in through that window in the dining room."

"Oh, no." Emma noticed that the box fan was on the floor. *Oh, why didn't I take it out of the window?* She went to the back door. She normally left the key to the deadbolt in a ceramic dish next to the back door. The key was gone.

After a few more words, the officers advised Emma to change the locks on all the doors. Then they left.

"He's on his way," she reported to Molly after calling the locksmith.

"You seem a little woozy," Molly said. "Were you sleeping?"

Emma shook her head. "No, I'm fairly sure that Shirley drugged me. Something was in that Turkish coffee."

"Wow," Molly said. "Are you feeling okay now?"

"Yeah, I think so," Emma said. "Although my head's still spinning a little."

Molly picked a cushion off the floor, the only one that wasn't completely destroyed, and put it on the sofa, motioning to Emma. They both sat leaning back against a pile of cushion stuffing. "So why do you think someone did this?"

"Shirley Parnell thinks Sarah did it. I don't know why they both thought *I* had the *Boke*."

"I know why." Molly's eyes were gleaming.

"Why?" Emma frowned.

"Because you *did* have it."

"What?"

Molly quivered with suppressed excitement. "It was in the slipcase of the *Space Trilogy*!"

"You're kidding!" Emma said.

"It was wedged in between the slipcase and…"

A pounding on the front door startled Emma. "Someone's at the door. It must be the locksmith."

While the man from A Lock and A Key installed new deadbolts on both doors, Molly told about her discovery.

"And you left the *Boke* in your house?" Emma whispered.

"Hidden in plain sight."

"I can't wait to see it!"

They both stared at each other.

"Well, well," Molly said. "So Sarah Bailey is in this Circle. It's starting to fit together. Didn't you see Dr. Parnell at Fred's that day you went to buy the Lewis books?"

"I did. She practically pushed me into the hydrangeas as she ran out the door. I wondered what she was doing there. And Sarah looked afraid. Dr. Parnell, I mean Shirley—she asked me to call her Shirley—must have gone there to demand the book, and Sarah told her she didn't have it."

"But she did." Molly pounded her fist into her palm. "She had it all along on a shelf in Fred's book annex. *He* didn't know it was there, or he wouldn't have sold it. So *he* isn't involved. Now *we* have it," she said in a low voice. "Why would she hide it where it could be sold?"

"Fred said he'd had the *Space Trilogy* forever, so he gave me a good price. I bet Sarah thought he wouldn't sell it before she could get the *Boke* out, take it to the Circle, and claim leadership."

Molly said, "She hid it because she knew that Shirley would try to get it."

"Shirley said that Bernard didn't leave a written directive saying who would be heir to the Circle."

"I'm sure he wouldn't put it in writing," Molly said. "Can you imagine it: 'I, Bernard Booth, Wizard of the Sherwood Forest Circle of Black Magic, do leave my grimoire, *A Boke of Secret Knowlege*, along with leadership of the Circle, to Dr. Shirley Parnell, Witch.' How would *that* stand up in court?"

Emma chortled. She looked at Molly. "I'm not withholding evidence any longer. The cops need to have the *Boke*."

Molly nodded. "I agree—right after I fit the note over the demon's face. Hey, want to go and look at it?" She looked toward the kitchen where the locksmith was installing a new deadbolt. "As soon as he's through."

"Tomorrow," Emma said. "If it's all right, I want to stay here tonight. I want to be in my home. Even if it's torn apart, it's mine." She hugged a slashed pillow to her chest. "But will the *Boke* be safe?"

"You forget—my house is guarded by giant beasts!"

The locksmith came up. "All finished," he announced. He handed Emma two keys. "This one's to the front door, and this one is to the back."

Emma thanked and paid him. She couldn't bear to look at her books any more tonight. Tomorrow she would figure out which books were salvageable. She felt chilled, but without the fan in the window, it was rather warm. She recognized that feeling. Often when she was nervous she tended to get cold and shake. She tried to brush pillow stuffing off her black linen skirt. Most of it stuck.

The two women sat together quietly, leaning against the back of the slashed sofa. After awhile, Emma said, "Are you sure you want to stay? I only have one bed, and the couch is not exactly in shape to be slept on."

"Do you want me to?"

"Yes," Emma said.

"Okay," Molly said. "We'll put a sword between us."

Emma laughed. She rose, held out her hand, and led Molly into the blessedly untrashed bedroom.

CHAPTER 32
Morning

Manley P. Hall, The Secret Teachings of All Ages: An Encyclopedic Outline of Masonic, Hermetic, Qabbalistic and Rosicrucian Symbolic Philosophy*, 1952, pebbled black cloth quarto, title in red rectangle on front cover. Comprehensive and illustrated coverage of occult subjects.*

Molly awoke to silence. No propeller tail banging against Batsky's crate, no sharp insistent barks from Dmitri. She turned over and felt half the bed made up, the cover pulled tightly over the sheets. She realized she was at Emma's house. How long had Emma been up? What time was it?

Molly had had a hard time falling asleep. The *Boke* had finally been in her hands, but she had to rush away. Now she was tempted to leap out of bed and run home, to make sure it was safe, then compare the handwriting to that on the note.

She and Emma had gotten into bed and lain back to back, not talking. Molly tried not to disturb her friend by changing position, but when Molly turned onto her back, Emma whispered, "I'm still shaking. Will you hold me?"

Molly reached out her right arm. "Yes, come here." And Emma nestled into Molly, head on Molly's chest. Molly stroked Emma's flannel-covered back, and before long Emma was asleep. Molly was not used to going to bed before one or two, and she had so much on her mind, and she could get up and find something to read, but she stayed because that was what she thought Emma needed. Little by little, her mind quieted, lulled by the other woman's even breathing and the soft feel of her head pillowed on Molly's shoulder. When Emma turned onto her side, Molly followed, holding her tight. Throughout the night one would turn and the other would follow.

∽∽∽

In the morning, she realized here she was in Emma's bed. Innocently, yet their friendship had changed. Would it go back to the way it was before, forgetting the tender night they had shared? Lying still, listening hard, Molly heard some bumping around in the house. She had slept in her T-shirt, socks, and underwear, so she got up and pulled on her jeans. She couldn't greet Emma without first running to the bathroom. After washing her face with lavender soap and swishing some mouthwash, she walked into the living room. Emma was on the floor, surrounded by books. She looked small and fragile in leggings and a long denim shirt. The big balls of stuffing had been swept up and the room looked a little less trashed. Slanting light came through the parted white curtains and threw dark and light streaks across the hardwood floor.

"Good morning," Molly said.

Emma looked up, tears in her eyes. "Hey," she said

softly.

Molly went over and touched her shoulder. Emma reached up and placed her hand over Molly's.

In a louder, angry voice, Emma said, "Why did they have to be so destructive?"

Molly shook her head and grasped Emma's hand.

"Some of these books I've had since grad school," went on Emma. "They're not valuable except to me. And some of these are signed first editions." She pulled her hand from Molly's and picked up a hardback of Marge Piercy's *Woman on the Edge of Time.* She held it open, and pages fell out. "Look," she said. "And it's signed to me. Makes me sick."

Molly nodded. "Me, too."

Emma gave her a half smile. "I made a pot of tea. Do you want some breakfast?"

"Sure. Let me know if I can help with anything."

They had sliced strawberries and bananas with vanilla yogurt and half a toasted English muffin apiece. They didn't talk much. When she finished eating, Molly said, "I'd better get back to the dogs."

"Oh my, are they in their crates?"

"No. And they can go out the dog door. It's just—they'll be worried about me."

Emma wiped her mouth as if hiding a smile.

Molly guessed it did sound odd, but she knew it to be true. "I'm also uneasy about the *Boke*. Do you want to come over and look at it?"

"In a little bit," Emma said. "Right now, I want to call my insurance company and straighten up the house. And then I have to go get my car. Will you drive me?"

"Of course," Molly said. "In an hour?"

At the door, Emma put her hand on Molly's sleeve. "You were so sweet to stay with me. See you in a bit."

She stood on tiptoe to lightly kiss Molly's cheek and quickly reached behind Molly to open the screen door, so there was nothing Molly could do but turn to leave. When she turned back around, the door was closed.

છૡઉ

"Guys," she cried out as Blavatsky and Dmitri jumped at the front door. "I missed you. Did you miss me?" She quickly glanced into the living room, relieved that everything was normal. The *Boke* was where she had left it. Blavatsky barked excitedly, then, having missed her nighttime and morning treats, ran to her crate. Dmitri hung back, wanting to smell his person who had been gone overnight, then herded Molly down the hall.

Dogs, fed their treats, settled down to munching salmon and sweet potato flavored dog food.

Molly took the manuscript to her desk and pulled a plastic bag out of the third drawer. Gently she grasped the note and laid it next to *A Boke of Secret Knowlege.* The paper looked the same age, although the manuscript had obviously been handled, since the right hand edges were soiled and worn thin. She carefully leafed through it, reading the intricate writing as best she could. She remembered Emma saying that Rowse's book on Simon Forman had samples of his writing. She would take it over to Emma's when she went to pick her up, and they could compare Forman's writing with the manuscript. When she got to the picture of the demon, she carefully lifted the note and laid it on the page. It fit perfectly where it must have lain for four hundred years. She cut two pieces of cardboard the size of the manuscript and put one on each side. She slipped it into the plastic bag and put it into her shoulder bag. Then she flung the bag over her shoulder, patted it as though to make it secure, and ran out of the house.

CHAPTER 33
Back to Sophia's

Nettie Colburn Maynard, Was Abraham Lincoln a Spiritualist? *1956, red cloth. Reminiscences of a medium who conducted séances with President Lincoln and the First Lady.*

Emma leaned on her vacuum cleaner and looked around her living room. After thoroughly vacuuming and dusting the entire house, she now felt that it was hers again. Well, almost. She shook her head. Molly would be there in a few minutes. While she waited, she decided to sit down and start on the inventory that the insurance company had asked for. She sat and began to write. A couch, an easy chair. Two end tables, a coffee table. One laptop, one printer. Six throw cushions. Two barrister bookcases with glass doors, five folding book shelves. Three picture frames with the glass broken.

   The books themselves were hardest to put a value on. How to put a price on her dog-eared, ragged, oversized second edition of *Our Bodies, Our Selves*? Or a yellow paperback of Beauvoir's *The Second Sex,* full of penciled notes? These had value for her, and most of them could never be replaced.

She put down her pen. She had delayed thinking about Molly and what was developing between them. What was she going to do?

Emma knew she was attracted to Molly. She liked her. She smiled as she thought of Molly's endearing traits, and her snoring had certainly been entertaining. She'd been so sweet to stay the night, although Emma was fairly sure it wasn't pure altruism.

Yes, affection was growing between them, but what else? When she thought about being with Molly, she felt excited, but also nervous. She picked up her slender blue pen, then laid it down again as she stared at the inventory list.

Then Molly was at her door, and Emma hastened to open it. "Come in. I think it's all mine again."

Molly looked around. "You did a lot."

"I had to do something. My nerves were jumping. Do you have the *Boke*?"

"Here it is. At last." Molly set her bag on the dining room table and placed the note and manuscript on the green and white tablecloth.

Emma picked up the plastic bag. "So, this little book—what would those people do to get it back?"

"Go ahead, take it out."

Emma lifted it out of the baggie. "*A Boke of Secret Knowlege,*" she said in a hushed voice.

"I saw where the note had to have been. And as Lewis described, there is a picture of a demon inside a circle on the page." Molly reached for the manuscript.

Emma kept her hand on it. "Just a minute." She ran her fingers over the cover and slowly opened the book. She turned with care the fragile pages that may have been written on by Simon Forman. She stopped when she saw the note. "This is where you think the note goes?"

"Yep."

Emma lifted the note and gazed at the demon. "Creepy. God, those tusks!" She picked up the note by two corners and carefully placed it back over the darkened rectangle. She drew in her breath. "Same paper. It was put in by whoever wrote the book."

"Go on, turn the page."

Pages of charts with weird symbols populated the rest of the text. "So this is what a grimoire looks like," murmured Emma.

"Let's compare the writing to Simon's."

"Hold on a minute." Emma picked up Rowse's book about Forman and turned to a photo of one of Forman's scrawled astrological charts. She turned to one of the hand-drawn charts in the *Boke*. They looked similar, had the same design. Unlike modern charts with their circles, Forman's were squares. "Oh my god, look, it's got to be by him. Look at this paragraph, and look here." She looked back and forth, searching out letters in common.

"Do you want to hide it here?" asked Molly.

"Yes, let's. They've already trashed my house, so I doubt they'll be back." Emma closed the *Boke* with the note on its proper page and placed Molly's cardboard backing around it. She slipped it into its plastic bag and placed it between two large art books.

They stood back and looked at the shelf for a second.

"Let's go get my car," Emma said.

On the way, Emma tried to formulate what she wanted to say to Molly. She finally began. "I am so lucky to have my own home. When they broke in, I was so shaken that someone came in without invitation. I wanted to be a *femme sole*—that's what they called a woman who lived and worked on her own in Renaissance England—for so long but was afraid."

"Why?"

Emma took a deep breath. "I was in a relationship for nearly twenty years. I met Gwen in grad school and we lived together before I finished my master's thesis. At first, we got along so well. We cared about each other. Then, although I never thought it would happen, she took over my life. I always saw myself as independent, so I didn't want to accept what was happening. We bought a house together. We got a cat, then another, then another until we had nine. They were our family. The house, the cats, her projects, took over my life. I was unhappy, but I felt afraid of breaking up the household, of going out on my own after so long, even while I dreamed of having a little house of my own."

She paused, looking at Molly. Seeing only sympathetic interest in the blue eyes, she continued. "Finally, I got the courage to leave when I found out she was trying to seduce her boss. In our house. She was always so jealous of me, didn't want me to have friends who weren't her friends, and then *she* wanted someone else. It infuriated me. Remember that snowstorm when we were snowed in for days?"

"Five years ago or so?"

Emma nodded. "Yeah. Gwen's car wouldn't start in the cold, so her boss Lillian gave her a ride home. They were used to going out for a drink after work together. They were already soused by the time I got home that night. To make things worse, I had a fender bender on the interstate coming home because my car slipped on the ice. Gwen had no sympathy for how rattled I was. They were in the laughing stage of drunkenness, and she said, 'Have a martini, we made a pitcher.' I thought maybe a drink would relax me, so I joined them, but I just felt more tense. So I left to take a bath." Emma hesitated.

Molly didn't say anything, but her brows drew together and she gave a minute shake of her head.

Emma plunged on with the story. "I could hear them through the walls. I couldn't *not* hear them! I ran more hot water to try to drown out their voices, but it didn't help. Lillian would say she had to leave, and then Gwen would start a long conversation to get her to stay. Finally, she said, 'Why don't you stay here tonight? The ice will melt tomorrow and we can go to work together.' Lillian agreed. We were snowed in, and Lillian ended up staying for three nights. I couldn't stand it. The flirtation!" *Oh, why am I telling her all this?* Emma looked at Molly. "I hate to burden you with my old stories."

"It's all right," Molly said quietly.

Emma gave a half smile. "I'm sorry to dump all this on you. It's not fair, you've been so nice to listen to me . . ." She let her voice trail off. *What will she think of me now? I've just unloaded all my bottled-up anger, bitterness, hurt. What kind of a person does that? A whiny, self-centered wimp, that's all I am. She's not going to want to have anything to do with me now.*

She drew herself up with a deep breath and looked directly at Molly. She saw no judgment in the blue eyes, only empathy. *She understands*, Emma thought. She rubbed her hands over her face. "Thank you for listening to me."

"I'm glad to listen," Molly said.

Emma drew another deep breath and let it out. "So—what I'm trying to say is—I'm finally happy with my life. Maybe someday I'll be ready to share it with someone else, but not yet."

Molly nodded. "Don't worry, Emma. I'm not trying to get into your life. I'm not ready to get involved with anyone either."

Emma leaned back and looked out the car window. She felt reassured. Yet a small part of her wondered how many women had seen that smile of Molly's. A line from a Joni Mitchell song went through her mind: "If you care, don't let them know/Don't give yourself away." Leaves on a few trees were turning yellow, a crape myrtle bush bloomed purple at the corner of a yard. Endings and beginnings. Emma thought, *I should feel relieved. She's giving me space. That's what I want, isn't it? So why do I feel sad? And where do we go from here?*

CHAPTER 34
A Circuitous Route

Ralph Shirley, Occultists & Mystics of All Ages, *1920, brown cloth with black lettering and embossing on front, black lettering on spine, black and white illustrations. Biographical sketches of Plotinus, Paracelsus, Swedenborg, and others.*

Molly pulled her van into the space next to Emma's Volvo station wagon and stopped. Only a couple of other cars were in the small parking lot. Sophia's looked as though it closed between lunch and dinner hours.

"You're awfully close," Emma said with a frown, peering at the space between the two cars. "To my car, I mean," she added.

They looked at each other. The silence seemed to stretch. Then Molly laughed.

After a moment, Emma laughed, too. "Thanks, Molly. Let's talk later about what we're going to do about the manuscript, okay?"

"Sure. Give me a call." Molly watched as Emma went to her station wagon, unlocked it, and got in with a wave. The Volvo exited the lot and disappeared.

Molly couldn't stop being attracted to Emma, but

she knew now not to act on it, not right away. Their friendship seemed to be moving quickly, becoming something more. Molly did want something more. Maybe not a *serious* relationship. But Emma was appealing. And so soft in cotton last night.

Molly decided to concentrate on her errands. First, she deposited a check into her credit union and then went to the natural foods market. Coming out with her kale, corn, and sweet potatoes for dinner, she noticed a dark green pick-up truck with a camper top and a large dent in the driver's side rear fender. She was almost certain that she had seen the same truck in the parking lot of the credit union. Was someone following her? Were they from Sophia's? She decided to go to the grocery store and see if the green truck would turn up again.

In the grocery, she ambled around even though she had only meant to get dog food and dog treats. She decided to treat herself to some salted caramel ice cream. After all, Blavatsky wasn't the only one who loved treats.

When Molly went back out to her van, she saw the green truck a couple of rows over. Determined to get a look at the driver or the license plate, she drove past that row, but the truck pulled out with a roar and a burst of black smoke from its exhaust. She glimpsed a ball cap with bushy red hair sticking out from under it behind the wheel. Before the truck disappeared, she tried to memorize the number on the license plate, but being terrible with numbers, she retained only a seven, a nine, and maybe a letter M. She did see that there was a chain around the license plate and a bumper sticker next to it, black and silver and spiky, vaguely suggestive of some heavy metal band. A worrying thought came to her: what if the driver was going to follow her to see where she lived and tear up her house like someone had Emma's?

She had told Emma that Blavatsky and Dmitri would keep anyone from breaking in, but what if it wasn't a common burglar, but someone evil who would stop at nothing to find the missing manuscript? They might hurt or even kill the dogs!

Stomach tight with growing worry, Molly drove through the Edgewood neighborhood, going down small streets, zig-zagging her way home. It occurred to her that the truck might come up behind her and trap her on a deserted street, but she got safely to Ormewood Avenue. Her heart sank: the green truck was a few cars behind her. She headed toward the nearest police station, a Craftsman bungalow near the zoo. She parked by the front door and rushed in.

"May I help you?" asked the young officer on duty.

"I'm being followed," Molly said in a gasping voice. She realized that it must sound overly dramatic. "It's a green pick-up truck. It doesn't belong to anybody I know."

"Where's the truck now? Is it outside?" The officer sounded matter-of-fact, as though she heard this kind of thing every day. She probably did.

Molly looked out the front window and shook her head. "I don't see it right now."

"Do you have any idea why someone would be following you?"

"My friend's place was broken into and searched last night. Everything was torn up. I'm afraid the driver of that truck might be the same person. They might want to see where I live and do the same thing." She put her palms down on the desk and caught her breath.

"Did she call the police?"

"Yes, they went to her house last night."

"Her address?"

When Molly gave Emma's address, the officer typed on a keyboard and squinted at the screen. "Do you have any idea what they were searching for?"

"It may be related to a case that Detectives DuBois and Richards are investigating."

The officer raised her eyebrows. "Homicide?"

Molly nodded.

"Your name?"

After Molly gave her name and address, the officer said, "Have a seat" and picked up her phone.

From where Molly sat, she could see out the front window, but the green truck wasn't where she could see it. But once she left here, it could—no doubt would—start following her again. Where could she go? And what about Emma? Maybe someone was following her as well.

Molly suddenly thought of something she could do. She walked back to the desk just in time to hear the officer on duty speak a number into the phone. Darn. If DuBois weren't answering, the plan wouldn't work.

"Was she available?" she asked the officer as soon as she put down the phone.

"No, but I left a message. You'd better stay here until the detective calls back," said the officer.

"Okay," Molly said. She sat and gazed at her phone's screen, scrolling down an uninteresting-looking list of e-mails urging her signature on a petition, offering free e-books, or 30% off clothing sales if you spent more than $150. She noticed the phone was getting low on power, so she went to her car and plugged it in. She glanced around, but didn't see the green truck. She remembered that Detective Richards had given her his card. She dug deep into her wallet, pulling out punch cards of four different coffee shops and frequent buyer cards of grocery stores and pharmacies. Finally she found two Atlanta police business cards. First she called Detective Richards and, as she thought, got voice mail. She hung up and sent a text to DuBois and Richards saying, "I have some evidence about the Booth murder. Emma's house was broken into last night, and I'm being followed. Could you meet me and Emma at Humdingers Coffee Shop on Moreland? Around 3:30?" That would give them thirty minutes. Surely homicide detectives checked their messages often. But what if they were on the scene of a fresh homicide?

Finally, she dialed Emma. "Emma, I hope you answer," she muttered. She whispered, "Yes!" to herself on hearing Emma's voice.

"Emma, I'm at the police station near the zoo."

"What? Why?"

"This creep tailed me from Sophia's, so I went to the police station. We have to give the *Boke* to the detectives right away."

"Thank god."

"Hey, I always said I would when I matched up the note with its book."

"You did," Emma replied.

Molly's phone chirped. A text from DuBois said she could meet them at 4:00. Molly quickly sent a thumbs-up reply. "I texted DuBois and she said she could meet us at Humdingers Coffee at 4:00. So can you bring the *Boke* and the note?"

"Why Humdingers?"

"I've got a fifty percent off coupon."

Emma laughed. "See you then."

When Molly went back into the station to wait, the

officer called out, "Hey, Detective DuBois called back. I told her you were being tailed and that it might be related to one of her cases. She said she was going to meet you."

"Oh, thanks. I got a text from her. I have something to give her that my friend's bringing to Humdingers."

At 3:45 Molly headed out. Aware that she might be followed again, Molly took a circuitous route to Humdingers, a busy neighborhood coffeehouse. Its feel was funkier than Oxygen's. There were big round tables and dilapidated couches along with little café type tables and molded plastic chairs. The only parking spot she found in the small L-shaped lot was at the back of the building. She pulled in and hopped out of the van just in time to see the green pickup swerve into the lot. Heart thumping, she quickened her step, longing to get inside to the safety of a public space with lots of people. She reached the back door as someone on her left rushed forward.

He reached the door the same time she did. She caught a flash of long red hair and an odd patch of baldness as an arm circled her shoulders and spun her around.

"Come on. Don't scream or attract attention or you'll be sorry," a voice hissed in her ear as a hard hand grabbed the nape of her neck. Terror washed down through her insides as something cold poked her waist—oh, god, a gun. Frozen, she felt her assailant spin her away from the glass door and shove her toward the green pickup truck.

CHAPTER 35
Where's Molly?

Jean Doresse, The Secret Books of the Egyptian Gnostics: An Introduction to the Gnostic Manuscripts Discovered At Chenoboskion, *1960, red cloth with gilt on spine. Dust jacket has white background with black and red lettering and a picture of an ancient manuscript in leather with ties. History of Gnosticism and the discovery of ancient texts including the complete text of the Gospel of Thomas.*

When Emma pulled into Humdingers's parking lot, her spirits lifted when she saw Molly's van parked in the back. She must have thrown off her follower, speeding through her secret way from the zoo to Moreland Avenue. Emma got out of her car and locked it, gripping her leather bag with the *Boke* and its note close to her body.

Inside, she didn't see Molly. Although Emma had been to Humdingers before, she hadn't been with Molly so didn't know where she preferred to sit. Emma herself liked the café tables, so she headed towards the one that was free. That area was sunny, sometimes intensely so. Maybe Molly was in the bathroom. Emma sat to wait instead of ordering since Molly had her fifty percent card.

After a few minutes, she went to the counter and asked, "Has a tall woman been in here? Short brown and gray hair?"

The young woman behind the counter said, "I don't know. That describes a lot of people."

What had she been wearing? When Molly got up that morning she'd had on jeans and a T-shirt. Was she still wearing it when she returned with the *Boke*?

"I think she was wearing jeans and a purple T-shirt that read: 'There's no such thing as too many books, just not enough bookshelves.'"

The coffee barista said, "That I would remember. I think she's a regular customer. Loves caramel latte, large."

"Yes! That's her!"

"Sorry, but I haven't seen her today."

Emma went outside and up to the van. It was locked and unoccupied. Strange. A group of people stood around the back door talking excitedly. A police cruiser pulled up. Could that be the detectives? Molly said they weren't picking up the phone, so maybe they sent uniforms to pick up the evidence she carried. Emma was disappointed at not seeing Detective DuBois and handing her the *Boke* personally. Although, she thought glumly, since Molly wasn't here to confess to picking up the note, Emma would receive any tongue-lashing that the police would dish out.

She waited for the police to park. Since there were no more parking places, the cruiser pulled behind a row of parked cars. Emma started toward the car. She saw a sandy-haired man with a guitar go up to the police officers. Two women and a man followed, staying a few steps back. The guitarist said, "It was obvious that she didn't want to go with them because the guy had a tight grip on her. She struggled a little when he pushed her in the truck, so I thought maybe it was a domestic thing. You know, like she left him or something and he and his friend had found her. That's why I called 911."

The other man, short with an Amish-type beard, said, "I saw this guy putting her in the truck when I drove up. The engine was on, so I knew there were two of them. She was standing with her feet planted like she didn't want to get in."

"He called her a bitch," a plump woman with large tattoos up and down her legs added.

Emma exclaimed, "Was she tall with short brown hair? Purple T-shirt?"

Everyone turned to her. "Yeah," the musician said.

A lanky uniformed officer stepped out of the passenger side. "Were you meeting her here?"

"Yes!" A corner of her mind recognized the sandy-haired man from a couple of weeks ago: he had been playing his guitar and just on the point of reaching out to put a bill in his cup, she had drawn back at the sight of milky coffee in the cup. He wasn't a busker after all. Giving him an embarrassed smile, she had stuck the bill back in her bag.

"Her name?" The officer asked.

"Molly O'Donnell."

The others started talking all at once. The officer said, "One at a time. Who called?"

"Me," said the guitarist, eager to tell his story. "I saw this woman get out of a van, walk to the back door, and then without even entering, all of a sudden, she was grabbed by this guy. She struggled a little, he told her she'd be sorry, he pushed her into a pickup truck, and they drove off. It was so quick, I didn't have a chance to say anything. I gave 911 the license tag though."

"What did he look like?"

"Youngish, long red hair. Redder than mine. Funny haircut."

The officers took statements from the other people who had seen her. He turned to Emma. "Is your friend married? In a relationship?"

"No. Neither." *Certainly not with a man*, Emma thought. "She called a little while ago and said somebody was following her."

"Did she say who?"

"No, but I may know why." She took a deep breath. "It's complicated. My house was broken into last night and I think whatever they were looking for, when they didn't find it at my house, they might think it's at hers. In fact, we're meeting Detective DuBois here to give her some evidence."

"Is that so? That changes things." He made a couple of quick calls. Then he asked for Molly's address and phone number.

Emma quickly looked up Molly's information and gave it to him. She held tight to the note and the *Boke*. But where was Molly?

CHAPTER 36
Unexpected Help

H. P. Blavatsky, Theosophical Glossary, *1892, blue cloth with gilt lettering on spine and front cover. Glossary of theosophical terms from many languages.*

Molly was squashed between two redheaded men on the bench seat of the green pickup. Pressed into the sweaty sleeve of the one who had grabbed her, she tried to lean away from him to protect the arm that hurt where he had gripped it. But whenever she tried to add space between them, the gun still poked her ribs. This small pickup was not intended for three adults to sit on the seat. Glancing down, she saw the gun in his left hand. A cold knot of fear squeezed her insides.

"Where's that book?" said the driver, roaring the motor, not looking at her.

"What you want is with the police." She drew a ragged breath and tried to keep her voice steady. "I don't have it. So why don't you let me go?"

"Bitch!" hissed the driver. "Now tell us where you live."

"No! I don't want you anywhere near my house!"

The other young man let out a sharp laugh like a

bark. "She thinks we care what she wants, Evan."

Evan said nothing, just gritted his teeth at the red light. When it turned green, he roared away. Molly tried to note as many details about the men as possible. Both appeared to be in their twenties. Evan looked older by a few years, though that might be because of his bushy red beard and the flaming hair that curled around his plaid shirt collar. A battered Braves cap sat low over his forehead. His hands, gripping the wheel, looked weather-reddened. His full mouth and bristling eyebrows were set in a scowl.

The one with the gun looked younger. Wiry, in tight black T-shirt and jeans, hair shaved on one side and falling in dirty red-gold waves to his shoulder on the other, his milk-white face looked clamped on bitter menace. He wore a silver-colored inverted pentagram pendant around his neck and a heavy silver bracelet that looked as though a small dragon had wrapped itself around his forearm. Multiple piercings adorned his ears. Sweat darkened the front and underarms of his T-shirt, its odor, reminiscent of cumin, made her wrinkle her nose.

Evan pulled onto a small street a few blocks from the coffee shop and pulled up behind a dirty white Impala.

"Get out." The pale man yanked her arm unnecessarily hard as he pulled her out with him, and she gave an involuntary yelp. "You wanted to get out, didn't you?" He gave another unpleasant bark of a laugh, and pushed her toward the Impala.

Evan said, "There's some rope in the trunk, Neil."

Rope? If Molly had felt scared before, she was terrified now. In spite of knowing never to get into a vehicle if nabbed, she had found herself in the truck. She would not get into the trunk of that car. She stiffened and tried not to let them move her forward. But they tied her hands behind her back, and Evan shoved her into the car's back seat. Both men got into the front. At least she didn't have the gun poking her. The Impala circled a block and headed away from Humdingers.

"You don't think they'll impound the truck, do you, Ev?" asked Neil.

"Nah, how could they? They'll be looking for it if anyone saw us. If they see it empty, they'll examine it and look around here."

Evan turned around. "Look, do you want to tell us where you live, or would you rather we take you out somewhere and make you tell us? It won't be pleasant." He sounded as though it might be pleasant for *him*.

Now Molly could smell fear rising from her armpits. "Atlanta Avenue. Near the police station." That might deter them. Her voice came out in a squeak. She was thinking fast. She could show them the set of books where the *Boke* had been hidden. But would they believe her that the *Boke* was gone? Or would they trash her house as they had Emma's? She'd think of something.

Evan eased onto Ormewood Avenue. Maybe when DuBois or Richards got her messages, they would go to her house. But they would have no reason to. They would go to Humdingers to meet Emma. She leaned her head on the window and watched the familiar houses go by. The rope rubbed her wrists. Would they untie her when they got to her house? "Turn left here," she directed.

There was her house. "This one." She saw Dmitri in the window. The curtain parted, revealing Blavatsky. Both were standing on the couch, their paws against the glass. They started to bark in unison.

"Damn! They're fucking monsters," said Neil, his

arm, white as an eel's belly, resting on the seat back. "I'll stay in the car."

Evan opened the back door and grabbed Molly's arm. She winced. It was starting to bruise. "Okay, we're gonna go in there and get that *Boke*. We see what we want, we'll let you go, so don't get any ideas. Neil," he directed, "get on the other side of her so nobody sees the rope." When Neil hesitated, Evan said, "Come on, chickenshit."

They escorted her down her long walkway, each pressing against her hard, gripping an arm each. Molly wondered what would happen if she bolted. Would the dogs break through the glass?

The dogs barked more vociferously, and Dmitri's paws were hitting the glass. But she didn't want him or Batsky hurt. Neil's gun was now hidden.

"Five seconds," muttered Evan.

"I need my hands free to get my keys." With her hands tied, her purse was hanging around her neck, weighing her down.

"Where are they?"

"In the front pocket."

Neil dug in her shoulder bag and pulled out the keys. Then he pulled her phone out, threw it on the walkway, and crushed it with his foot. She winced, almost feeling the blow. They stepped up onto the front porch, and Neil gave the keys to Evan, who put one in the lock, cursed, and tried another one. "Name o' Uriel!" muttered Evan, holding the keys up like spears coming out of his fist. "Which one?"

"The one next to the big black car key goes in the top."

Evan unlocked the dead bolt.

"Now the one next to it goes to the lower lock."

Loud barking sounded on the other side of the door. Neil backed off the porch onto the walkway.

"Hi, guys," said Molly, voice shaky, talking through the door as she always did. "What are my guys doing?" Her voice wasn't ringing out the way it usually did when she was glad to see the dogs. To Evan, she said, "With my hands behind my back, I can't hold the dogs back or pick up the book."

Evan said, "I'm not scared of dogs like my brother is."

"Fuck you," Neil said. "I had to get stitches."

"I know, I know. Twenty-three stitches." Evan laughed. "On your butt!"

Neil's pale skin took on the color of a cooked beet. "I gave that coonhound what he had coming!"

Evan's laugh halted. "You'll go to hell for shooting Diablo."

Neil started to laugh, but it came out in a squeak like boy sopranos approaching their last concert.

As Molly pushed the door slowly open with her shoulder, two competing dog noses pushed out.

Neil took a step back. "Don't let those fucking dogs out."

"We can slip past them," Molly said.

"You can control them, right?" Evan asked.

For answer, Molly said, "Get back, guys!" With her elbow she eased the door open wide enough to slip in, but stopped when she heard a female voice.

"Molly! This fell in my yard from *your* tree. If it had hit my car—"

Molly turned automatically to see her neighbor, Angie, carrying a five-foot-long limb. The next thing she knew, one hundred and fifty pounds of dog pushed her aside as Dmitri and Blavatsky charged out, barking for all they were worth.

Neil's high voice yelled, "Stop that dog!" as Dmitri charged after him. Angie jumped off the walkway, the limb raised in front of her like a shield as the terrified man and Dmitri sped past, Dmitri barking and Neil screaming, "Help!"

Molly swiveled to see Evan lying on the porch, half in, half out the front door with Blavatsky standing over him, growling and barking in his face. He was yelling, "Get away! Get your dog away from me!"

Her neighbor cried out. "God, Molly! What's going on?"

"Angie, untie me!"

Angie dropped the limb and hurried over. Taking a pair of pruners from her pocket, she cut the rope that bound Molly's wrists. "That your phone?" she said, pointing to the smashed phone on the walkway.

"Yes! Call the police! Hurry!" yelled Molly.

Angie's eyes opened wide as she pulled out her own cell phone.

Meanwhile, Neil was scrambling from the Impala's hood onto its top as Dmitri circled the car, jumping up on its sides, barking like a fire alarm, and pausing to sniff each tire as he ran around it. "Evan, you ass, why'd you lock the car?"

Molly noticed Evan squirming away from Blavatsky. She picked up the limb that Angie had dropped.

"You stand up, and I'll knock the shit out of you!" she yelled, brandishing the limb over him. He shrank away from her, curling up like a snail. Blavatsky eyed the stick but held her stance over Evan. Somehow she knew Molly wasn't trying to start a game of fetch.

A police siren joined the din, and a second later a police car rounded the corner and screeched to a stop behind the Impala. The officers who piled out stared at the sight of Neil being held at bay on top of a car by a giant wolfhound.

As an officer approached Molly, she cried out, "These bastards kidnapped me!"

"Put the stick down, lady," he said.

She dropped it. No need getting shot for wielding a weapon. The other officer hollered, "Call off your dogs!"

She called Dmitri and Blavatsky, gripped their collars, and got them both inside. She and the dogs watched through the window, all three breathing fog on the glass while the officers handcuffed the brothers. Once they had them in the police car, Molly went outside in time to see another police cruiser and Detective DuBois's black Ford pull up. After DuBois huddled with the police officers a moment on the sidewalk, she came to the door.

"Stay, guys. Be good dogs."

"Ms. O'Donnell, we need you to come downtown," DuBois said in a stern voice.

"Let me lock up the house and give my dogs treats."

"Be quick about it," DuBois snapped.

Molly, not taking time to answer, raced to the treat box. She fed each dog a large treat, placing her hands on the side of each dog's face and saying, "You good, good dogs! You wonderful, sweet little, good little dogs!" In front of Blavatsky's cage was the washcloth that Molly had carelessly draped over the side of the bathtub that morning. She grabbed it while Blavatsky munched on the peanut butter-flavored bone.

When she got into the back seat of the Crown Victoria, she cried out, "Emma!"

"Oh, Molly! Thank goodness!" Emma was in the

back seat, looking more worried than Molly had ever seen her. She threw her arms around Molly and hugged her tight. Molly shrank back in pain.

"Sorry," Emma said, loosening her arms.

"No, no, I'm okay. Just—he grabbed me by the arm and his gun poked me in the ribs." She rubbed her side, then asked, "You've got the *Boke*?"

"Yes!" Emma clutched her purse.

Molly relaxed a little.

Emma gave her a softer hug. "What's that in your hand?"

Molly looked down at the dirty white washcloth. "Meant to throw it in the laundry," she muttered and draped it over her purse. They silently rode to police headquarters, sitting close beside each other. In the rear view mirror Officer DuBois's face was drawn, her lips, wearing dark red lipstick, appeared stuck tight together. What would happen to them for withholding evidence?

CHAPTER 37

It's Not Over Yet

F. E. Ormsby, Planets and People, The Great Year-Book of the Heavens: All About the Stars for 1896, *1895, brown cloth with black lettering and embossing on front cover. Astrological charts for every week in 1896 along with advice on subjects such as birth, marriage, business, and physiological subjects. Includes ephemeris for 1896.*

Emma and Molly sat in Detective DuBois's office in two straight chairs, Emma with the plastic baggie containing *A Boke of Secret Knowlege* on her lap. She held it tight with both hands. She felt Molly's tension from across the few inches that separated them. Molly was still breathing hard. Emma wanted to pat her back and make soothing noises.

"So," said Detective DuBois, a satisfied smile on her face. Her office chair squeaked as she leaned forward. "I want to thank you both for helping us catch the two guys who broke into Ms. Clarke's house. They admitted they did it." The smile dropped off the detective's face, leaving it square and stern. "However, you both have some explaining to do. About why you were withholding evidence from the police."

"It was me, Detective. I'm the one who kept that note. Emma urged me to give it to you," Molly said.

Emma said quickly, "Detective DuBois, we know we shouldn't have kept that note. We've got it right here." She rose from her chair and placed the plastic baggie on the detective's desk. "This is the book we were looking for, and the note that Molly took that day of the estate sale, the note that was on the floor next to Buck Hubbell's body. It fell out of this book."

DuBois read the title slowly, squinting. "*A Boke of Secret Knowlege by a Learned Doctor.*" She pronounced "boke" with a long "o."

"It's pronounced 'Book,'" Emma said. "Back when it was written, spelling hadn't been standardized—"

Detective DuBois held up her hand, and Molly shook her head at Emma. But then Molly said, "The note is in its right place in the book. It's a warning, so—"

Emma interrupted, saying, "This is what those men were looking for when they trashed my house and took Molly."

Detective DuBois raised her eyebrows. They were thick and dark, Emma noticed, much darker than her hair.

DuBois fixed her eyes on Molly and said, "And you thought it was a good idea to withhold evidence because—why?"

Molly said, "I wanted to find the book. Re-unite the ephemera with the book it came out of. You know, ephemera as in ephemeral, things not intended to last."

DuBois nodded too slowly as though she had just heard something particularly lacking in sense. "And that's why you kept the book and the note from the police."

"But we weren't withholding the book, because we didn't have it, and I told Emma that, as soon as we found it, we would turn over the note and the book."

"I don't have to tell you," said DuBois, "that what you did could be serious."

Molly dropped her head. "I know." Her voice sounded contrite. Emma, however, knew that Molly would do it all over again.

DuBois grabbed the baggie and Emma cringed, afraid she would damage the *Boke*. But she carefully slid it out, holding it gently. "Where's the warning?"

Molly lunged for the *Boke*, and DuBois pulled it to her chest.

"About halfway through," Molly and Emma said at once.

Inwardly Emma thought, *careful, careful*, but she didn't dare say it out loud. She watched DuBois slowly turn the thin pages. When the detective got to the note, she gingerly picked it up.

"See, we thought, that, um, that warning note could be an important piece of evidence," Molly said.

Oh, why doesn't she shut up, Emma thought. *She should have stuck to her story of matching the note and book.*

But DuBois studied the note. She looked at Emma. "And this is how old?"

"You see, Simon Forman was a physician and astrologer in the Renaissance who delved into magic and summoned spirits, as did others: John Dee, Giordano Bruno—"

DuBois put up her hand in a "stop in the name of love" gesture.

"Probably sixteenth or seventeenth century," Emma said.

DuBois said, "Amazing it has lasted so long."

Emma wanted to tell about how it had been passed down through generations, but she decided she'd better just answer questions.

Like a border collie giving the eye to a sheep, DuBois stared at Emma. "And you said you have more information for us."

"That's right," said Emma. "I was also forced into a car and taken to my own house by someone who was after this same book, and it was for the same reason these men kidnapped Molly."

DuBois snapped, "Who did this?"

Emma told about her evening with Shirley Parnell. DuBois listened in silence, and then said, "We need your help." She explained what she wanted them to do.

Leaving the police station, Molly and Emma waited for the officer who was going to take them back to Humdingers, where both their cars waited.

"Are you sure you still want to be part of this?" asked Molly. "After all, I'm the one who got us into it. If I hadn't picked up that note—"

"If I hadn't gone down to the basement when the sign clearly said, 'Do Not Enter'—" Emma said. "I said, 'I'm in.'" She gave Molly's arm a squeeze.

Molly winced.

"Oh, sorry. I forgot." Emma dropped her hand. "We need to talk about what DuBois asked us to do."

Molly said, "I still have a fifty percent off coupon for Humdingers."

CHAPTER 38
A Gathering of Witches

Jacobus Sprenger & Henrich Kramer, translated and edited by Montague Summers, Malleus Maleficarum, *1928, buckram cloth with vellum spine, hand made untrimmed paper, limited edition of 1,275 numbered copies. Originally published in 1487 in Germany, this was the major text for those persecuting persons for witchcraft.*

Molly dreaded making this phone call, but she had promised. "I've decided I'd like to buy all of the books," she said, cradling her phone in her left hand while giving a treat to Blavatsky with her right. The wolfhound took it in her jaws delicately and trotted away to her crate, her preferred place to enjoy treats in private.

"You're sure?" Dr. Booth's voice held a frown. "You went over them pretty carefully when you were here. What made you change your mind?"

Uh-oh, thought Molly. *Maybe he sold the rest to some other dealer.* The idea piqued her competitive bookseller's soul. "I'm sure I want them," she said in a firm voice. "When can I come over to finalize the deal?"

"Ah—tomorrow night?" Dr. Booth sounded hesitant.

"Tonight would be better for me."

"Okay," he said. "Six o'clock? I've got to get Kelly to the high school by seven-thirty."

They agreed, and Molly clicked the phone off. "Okay, we're on for six tonight." She put the phone down. "Your turn, Emma."

"She's got to think this is odd after our last episode." Emma punched in a number. "Why do I feel like I'm getting ready to tiptoe around a cobra?"

"Courage, old girl," Molly said, winking. Emma grimaced.

"Dr. Parnell—Shirley?" Emma said. Her voice sounded more confident than Molly expected. "It's Emma Clarke. Listen— don't hang up. I found what you're looking for. It was in a boxed set I bought from Fred." She held the phone away from her ear, and Molly heard a torrent of words on the other end. Emma put the phone back to her ear and continued. "I know, I know. But when I was at dinner with you, I didn't know it was there. My friend Molly found it. She's got it, and she's taking it back to Dr. Booth tonight."

Molly fidgeted. She couldn't hear what Shirley was saying now, and Emma was listening and not saying anything. Then Emma burst out: "No! It was in Dr. Booth's house, so it belongs to him. I don't want any more trouble about it. I don't care what it can or cannot do. I don't want to be in the middle of anything with you and Sarah. I just want to get rid of the *Boke*." Another long pause on Emma's end, making Molly's hands tremble, causing the bag of treats to clack. The chewy bones knocking against each other brought both dogs to her knee. She thought, *what is Shirley Parnell saying?* Emma said, "Six o'clock tonight. If you think it belongs to you, you can take that up with Dr. Booth."

Molly looked at her with approval. "You did a great job." She noticed Blavatsky and Dmitri, twin heads with hopeful eyes. She gave them each a treat.

"Thanks," Emma said. She laid down the phone and sank onto Molly's sofa. "It was creepy talking with her again." She shuddered. "And for her to act like she hadn't drugged and kidnapped me."

"So she'll be there?"

"She said she would."

"Now to call Sarah. Are you sure you want to?"

"Not really, but I don't have much choice, do I? Do you have her number?"

"No, but I have Fred's." Molly scrolled for Fred's name. "Let's see, I have a cell and home number. Hey, I have an idea! Since we haven't had any dealings with Sarah, why don't I call Fred on his cell? I'll think of something about the book fair to talk to him about. While we're talking, you call the house phone, and if Sarah answers, give her a message for Fred. Say that you found something in the *Space Trilogy* and you're not sure if it belongs there."

"But that's not what Detective DuBois asked us to do."

"She didn't dictate what to say. She just told us to get them all together in the Booth house basement. Think about it. Sarah doesn't know that we know about her involvement."

"You're right. I'll do it."

Once Molly was in a conversation with Fred about how many tables and chairs to order, Emma called. When Sarah answered, she said, "Hi, Sarah, is Fred available? This is Emma Clarke. I want to ask him about a booklet that I found in the *Space Trilogy*. Could he call me?"

Molly tried to listen to what Fred was telling her about the screwed-up table order and also hear what Emma was saying. It wasn't easy.

"Oh, well, then," Emma said. "Tell him that I found out that it was part of the library at the Booth home." She paused to listen. "It was in Mr. Booth's catalog. Yes, his grandson Dr. Booth is selling them. Tonight, as a matter of fact. I'm going over there with Molly, you know Molly?" A pause. "You want to meet us there? I guess that would be all right. We're meeting him at six."

Emma punched the button ending the call and threw down the phone. Once Molly had ended her call, Emma said, "Well, she sure was anxious to come over."

Molly said, "I'll bet! Let's get our plan together, all right?"

"I'm scared, Molly. We're going to be there by ourselves. Anything can happen."

Molly gave her a smile and a pat on the shoulder that turned into a brief squeeze. "We'll be fine."

Emma nodded. "Okay," she said. But she didn't look reassured.

೧೨೬೨

Molly and Emma pulled up in front of the Booth house at ten minutes until six. Dr. Booth was waiting at the door. "Come on in," he said in his usual irritated voice, closing the door behind them. "I have plans for later in the evening, so this can't take long." He turned and started for the hall.

"It won't," Molly said to his back, but thinking, *this*

will only work if everyone is punctual.

His daughter Kelly was on the sofa, texting. She wore black leggings, a black lacy top, and soft-looking black slippers. Her hair was caught up in a bun with tendrils waving out of it. She looked a little more dressed up and slightly less bored than usual.

"You've met my daughter Kelly before?" said Dr. Booth. "She has a school thing this evening we've got to go to."

"Hi, Kelly," Molly said.

Kelly shot them a somber glance and continued texting.

Going downstairs reminded Molly again of discovering Buck, and she shuddered. But her spirits lifted when she looked up and around at the shelves of books that covered one wall. And they'd soon be hers. More than selling them, she wanted to look at them, turn their pages, feel their bindings, dip into them, and read choice tidbits of what people in times long gone believed about the world and their part in it.

She watched Emma run her fingers along a row of leather spines. Her face looked as though she were listening to the books.

"So what's your best offer?" Dr. Booth's nasal voice cut into her thoughts.

"How about five thousand for the lot?"

Dr. Booth pursed his lips. "That's too low. I think they're worth at least thirty K."

"I looked them up," countered Molly, "and I think that many of them are worthless except as curiosities. Many are quite common, and others are in poor condition."

Dr. Booth started to speak, but his head jerked up as a loud crack resounded. Molly felt her stomach lurch as a section of the book-filled wall tilted towards them.

Emma backed away toward the stairs.

The book wall stopped moving as though it were momentarily stuck, then swiveled all the way open, and Shirley Parnell stepped out.

Molly had never met her, but knew at once who she was. Shirley stood at least six feet, an inch taller than Molly. She wore a black thigh-length tunic, black tights, and tall black boots, and carried a large leather cross-body messenger bag. Her sleek blonde hair seemed to give off a pale light of its own.

"Who are you?" exclaimed Dr. Booth.

Shirley ignored him and nodded at Emma, then turned to Molly, who could not help feeling a churning of fear in her gut. The woman gave off a definite air of menace.

"See here," Dr. Booth said. "How did you get in here? What do you think you're doing?"

Ignoring him, Shirley said in a low voice, "I believe you two have something for me. You brought it, didn't you? So give it to me," she said, looking at Emma, then Molly. Her eyes bored into Molly's. "It's rightfully mine." She took a step closer.

Molly stepped back, almost bumping into Dr. Booth.

"What are you women talking about?" he asked.

"Emma said you had it," said Shirley. "Now give me that book." She reached into her shoulder bag.

Just then, footsteps sounded on the stairs, and Sarah Bailey stepped down. Molly gasped in spite of herself. Gone was the quiet, smiling bookseller's wife—in her place was a Queen of the Night, arms encircled with twisted silver bracelets carved in intricate designs. Her grey hair flowed over her shoulders, which were covered with a deep purple shawl. Her skirt was black with metal rivets. She wore no makeup, which somehow made her pale face more challenging than Shirley's. She was followed by Kelly, who stood behind her and gazed as if star-struck at this hippy-turned-glamorous witch.

Shirley glared at Sarah. "What are you doing here?"

Sarah hissed, "Why are you here?"

"Now, now, girls—" Dr. Booth started to step between them. Sarah whirled towards him and her skirt swung out. The metal rivets flashed in the light. She held up her hand, palm toward him in the stop sign gesture. Dr. Booth stopped as if hitting an invisible wall. "Timmy," she said in a soft tone. "This doesn't concern you. You could have learned Magic, too, Timmy. But no, you were so self-righteous."

"What Granddad did gave me the creeps."

Timmy? Molly thought.

"But it didn't stop you from going from understudy to star in *Brigadoon* in high school. Because the lead mysteriously lost his voice."

"I didn't want it that way."

Sarah clicked her tongue. "Lucky for me. So now, give me the *Boke*."

"I have no idea what you are talking about," Dr. Booth said.

"Emma said she was going to give it back to you."

Shirley turned her gaze to Molly. "You've got it, don't you? I thought it was that elderly pixie Clarke. But it was you all along." She stepped toward Molly, her hand still in her bag. "Now give it to me."

"I . . ." Molly looked from Shirley to Sarah. "I don't have it."

"What?" cried Sarah and Shirley at the same time.

"She's telling the truth," Emma said. "Molly doesn't

have it. I do."

"You!" Again both women exclaimed at once.

Emma said, "Yes, I have *A Boke of Secret Knowlege by a Learned Doctor*. Possession of which bestows leadership of the Circle that has extended in an unbroken line in the Harford family from the time of its author, the alchemist and astrologer Simon Forman."

Shirley beamed. "It's true. My research shows it."

Sarah gave her a withering glance and muttered, "Pedant."

"So," continued Emma, "*A Boke of Secret Knowlege* came to Bernard Booth, Dr. Booth's grandfather. He was the leader of a circle of practitioners of Ceremonial Magic that has been in existence for over 400 years."

"This is crazy!" sputtered Dr. Booth. He looked as if he was afraid to move lest he be stopped again. "He might have dabbled a little to help people out from time to time." His forehead was gleaming with sweat and his voice sounded unsure.

"It was more than dabbling," muttered Kelly Booth. She stepped off the stairs.

Sarah whispered, "Shhhh!" But Kelly walked to Sarah's side, brushing against the metal rivets and making them clack.

Sarah added, "And the leadership of the Circle has been handed down in a direct line of Harfords from the original Lord Alfred."

"You're not in the direct line!" said Shirley. "I too am descended from Lord Alfred, and I have as much of a claim by blood as you. But Bernard named me his successor."

"You seduced him," said Sarah in that low, cold voice.

Shirley lifted her chin. "Bernard and I shared a

special relationship. The Circle teaches that our bodies are sacred, and that we should not be ashamed of them. We worshipped—yes, worshipped—one another bodily here in this place." Her voice lowered. "You were only his little cousin with your thrift-store blouses and those tacky metal studs. But *I* was his lover."

Sarah laughed. "You think you're the first woman—or man—that Bernard had a special relationship with? Even above and beyond the customary way of sealing an initiate?"

Kelly looked at Sarah, eyes shimmering, while Shirley looked razors at them.

Sarah broke the silence, looking at Shirley. "You are pitiable. We laughed about how you tried to get him to marry you so you would be his heir. But you know that I have the greater power. I've been practicing since I was a teenager." Sarah turned to Emma. "Emma, you brought *A Boke of Secret Knowlege*. Now give it to me."

"She brought it to *me*!" said Shirley. "She called me and said she would bring it here."

"Did she now?" Sarah looked at Emma, then Molly. "You tried to double-cross us both. You two pitiful rationalists."

Shirley's face was in a frozen fury. She reached into her bag and pulled out a gun.

Dr. Booth shouted, "Kelly! Get under the stairs."

Kelly only pulled closer to Sarah.

"Don't any of you move," Shirley said, teeth gritted. "I doubt even *your* Magic can push back a bullet." She quickly thrust her chin in Emma's direction. "Emma, give me the *Boke*." She glared at Sarah. "If you try to do any harm to it, you will be shot before you begin."

"I would not harm the *Boke*," said Sarah. "Only a

crass creature, such as yourself, would even consider such a thing." Drops of saliva hovered in the corners of her mouth.

"Emma, I'm waiting," said Shirley.

Emma took a step forward.

Behind her a woman's husky voice said, "Drop the gun."

CHAPTER 39
Secrets Revealed

Dion Fortune, The Cosmic Doctrine, *1966, grey cloth with silver lettering on spine. Dust jacket has black background with white lettering and picture of the cosmos. Teachings received from a highly evolved being on cosmic law, laying the foundation for esoteric knowledge.*

Emma looked up to see Detective DuBois descending the stairs, followed by two uniformed officers. Everyone froze.

"Put it down now," Detective DuBois said in staccato tones. "On the floor," she added as she reached the bottom, her gun pointed at Shirley.

Shirley looked as though she didn't know what to do. She looked at Sarah, her enemy, as if in a mute plea to save them through magic. She slowly bent and laid the gun on the concrete floor.

"Now push it toward me with your toe."

Shirley did so with her booted foot.

DuBois crouched to pick up the gun and handed it to one of the other officers.

Emma looked at the basement's occupants from Dr. Booth, who gaped with open mouth, his glasses askew—to Kelly and Sarah, leaning close together, silver and blonde heads almost on a level—to Shirley, whose sharp face stared at DuBois in sullen defiance—to Molly, who looked pleased.

DuBois asked, "Who has the book?"

Emma felt the searing heat of so many eyes looking at her. "I do," she said, almost whispering. She held the baggie out to DuBois, who seized it and raised it over her head.

"Now, who killed for this little tome?" DuBois asked.

A moment of heavy silence followed her words. Then a tumult arose of overlapping voices.

Shirley pointed toward Sarah and shouted, "She did it!"

"You liar! You killed him yourself! Just the sort of thing you'd do," Sarah burst out.

"You know I was nowhere near here! I couldn't have been. I *work* for a living!"

Kelly hunched her shoulders and looked down, rubbing her bare arms. Dr. Booth's face had paled, and his air of professional arrogance had dropped off him, leaving a dejected, weary, and confused gray-haired man. He was no taller than his teenage daughter, at whom he glanced with a worried frown.

"One at a time." DuBois's voice cut through the tumult.

When quiet prevailed, she continued, "Everyone, state your name and where you were the Friday of the estate sale at ten a.m. when I point at you." She pointed at Shirley. "Starting with you."

Shirley took a deep breath. "I am Dr. Shirley Parnell. I teach religious studies at the university. That Friday, I had office hours from 10:00 to 1:00." She paused.

"Three students can corroborate that fact."

DuBois indicated Dr. Booth.

"I'm Tim Booth—Dr. Timothy Booth—and I haven't a clue what's going on. I was filling a cavity that morning when I got a call from the estate sale people about a body being found. They said to come over to the house right away. I had to ask the other dentist to finish." He shifted and shook his head. "Terrible, just terrible."

DuBois pointed at Kelly.

"I don't know anything either," the girl said. She pushed a long strand of hair back over her ear.

"Name?"

"Oh, I'm Kelly Booth. Can my Dad and I go now? I'm gonna be late for the dance recital."

DuBois said quietly, "Not yet. I'll need a signed statement from you and your father. And, by the way, you haven't said where you were that Friday morning at ten o'clock."

Kelly said, "School, of course."

"And you," the detective said to Sarah. "Your name and where you were Friday morning."

Sarah drew herself up, the corners of her thin mouth tucked in. "I'm Sarah *Harford* Bailey, and I think I was helping my husband catalog books. That's what I do most days."

DuBois looked at Molly.

"Molly O'Donnell, bookseller." Emma felt a surge of pride at Molly's confident stance and strong voice. "I was upstairs looking at books."

DuBois turned and looked at Emma.

Emma felt her usual panic at being suddenly the center of attention. Her throat closed up, and her hands began to shake. *Get hold of yourself, Em*, she told herself.

You're a grownup now. Been one for a long time. She dug her thumbnail into the cushioned part of her middle finger on her left hand, her usual technique for quelling nervousness in front of people.

"I'm Emma Clarke," she said clearly. "I discovered the body."

"Now," DuBois said, "Who here is a member of this Circle?"

Shirley gasped. "How did you—?"

DuBois ignored her. "And keep in mind that if you're lying, we will find out."

Sarah and Shirley slowly raised their hands. A slight shake of Sarah's head at Kelly didn't escape Emma's eyes, nor, she hoped, the detective's.

DuBois looked at Kelly.

"No," Kelly said.

"I told you I don't even know about this Circle," Dr. Booth said. His voice faltered.

"Sarah, how did you come to have possession of this little book?" The detective raised the baggie again.

"What do you mean?" Sarah's face looked blank.

"We know where it was hidden. Among your husband's books."

Shirley broke in. "That's right! You took it and hid it. It was supposed to live here in the basement. To always be here, ready for when the Circle met."

At the accusing glances, she continued, defiance in her voice. "I don't care who knows that I was in the Circle! We have nothing to be ashamed of. Even Wicca is a recognized religion now. I teach it in my 'Introduction to American Spirtualties' course."

"Wicca," Sarah snorted.

"Anyway, shortly before he made his transition, Bernard visited my class. The students loved him." She laughed, but broke off abruptly. Emma thought her eyes blinked rapidly for a moment. Shirley continued as she spun toward Sarah. "None of us has anything to be ashamed of here—except the person who killed in order to take the *Boke*."

"Shut up, Shirley. You wanted the *Boke*, too. You had to have it to make your claim look legitimate," Sarah said.

"But I didn't break in here and take it and kill some little book dealer!"

"He was a book *thief*. We all—all the book dealers—knew about him, didn't we?" Sarah looked at Molly and then Emma, including them with herself.

"Stealing books is reprehensible," DuBois said in a dry voice, "but it doesn't warrant capital punishment."

Emma felt her own lips twitch. *Good thing, or I'd be on Death Row right now.* Molly looked at her and gave an almost imperceptible wink.

DuBois crossed her arms and said evenly, "We know the murder is tied into this little book. All of you here wanted it, isn't that true?"

"It's rightfully mine!" said Shirley.

Emma didn't want to think of herself as included, but she and Molly had wanted to find it.

"Not me," said Dr. Booth. "How could I if I didn't even know about it? It was just one of the books I inherited, so I didn't particularly want it, except maybe to sell." He looked down at his watch. "Listen here. Can Kelly and I take off? Her dance recital starts at 8:00 and she has to get there early. I promise we will come into the station tomorrow and give a statement."

"I'm afraid not," DuBois answered. "I need you to stay a little longer."

"Am I under arrest?" he asked, making a weak

attempt at sarcasm.

"The book *was* in your possession. An estate sale was going on upstairs that didn't include the books in the basement. Yet someone found their way downstairs. Would you have hidden yourself here to make sure that no one found that one book? And would you be willing to kill to keep anyone from taking it?"

"I didn't even know that book existed, dammit!" The dentist was managing to work himself up into a minor tirade. "You can't keep me here unless I'm under arrest."

"True." The detective unclipped handcuffs from her belt. "So I'm going to make an arrest."

Gasps went up all around.

"Sarah Harford Bailey, you are under arrest for the murder of Buckminster Hubbell."

Sarah stepped back, black skirt swirling. "What— are you insane?"

DuBois snapped the handcuffs on her wrists.

"No!" Kelly cried out. "It wasn't her."

Dr. Booth stepped forward. "Come on, Kelly, let's go. They can't keep us here."

Kelly stepped in front of Sarah, throwing out her arm protectively. "It was me!" she screamed.

"No, Kelly!" Sarah said. "Don't try to save me, go on to your recital. Go!"

Kelly didn't move. "I wasn't at school. I was with Aunt Sarah. We came over here to make sure no one came down into the basement."

Sarah shook her head, and her mouth framed the word *No!*

"Sorry, Dad," Kelly went on, her pale face flooding with color, "but I'm going to be initiated into the Circle."

"What! You—you knew about it? How?"

Kelly's words tumbled out like a leaf going over the rapids. "We saw him taking books from the shelf and stuffing them into his jacket. And Aunt Sarah saw him grab the *Boke* and made him drop it. They both reached for it and they were struggling on the floor, and he grabbed her around the throat. I saw the old cast iron fireplace set and I picked up the poker and hit him on the head." A little sob escaped her lips. "I didn't think— I was trying to protect Aunt Sarah." She covered her mouth with her hands.

"Nonsense," Sarah said, but her voice shook. "She's trying to take the blame. I was the one who hit him."

"Sarah, no," blurted Kelly.

Dr. Booth turned to Sarah. "You—you hateful, wicked—*witch!* You dared to involve my daughter in that filthy, corrupt—!" He started to throw himself at her, but was restrained, not by Sarah's invisible wall, but by a uniformed officer, who quickly stepped forward and seized him by both arms.

Sarah began to laugh. Her laugh was soft at first, silvery as mercury, and then grew louder, almost hysterical. Everyone became quiet. "Yes, Timmy," she managed to say, "That's exactly what I am. A witch." She pointed at Shirley. "And so is she." Her index finger moved in Kelly's direction. "And she's going to be a witch, too—a fine one. And there's nothing you can do about it. *Nothing!*"

Kelly threw her arms around Sarah and hugged her tight.

"Oh, yes I can!" Dr. Booth sputtered.

Sarah smiled and said, "But not for long. And she's next in line to lead the Circle."

Shirley snorted. "Her? Bernard would laugh!"

Kelly smiled smugly.

DuBois handcuffed Kelly and then Shirley.

"Why me?" Shirley snapped. "That child confessed!"

"For kidnapping." DuBois turned to the officers. "Let's get everyone out of here now." DuBois said to the three under arrest, "You have the right to remain silent . . ." as she led them up the stairs. Dr. Booth followed close behind, shoulders slumped.

Emma sought out Molly, who came quickly toward her and grasped her hands.

"Oh, god, Molly—" Emma began.

"Shhh." Molly reached inside her collar and detached a small microphone.

Emma said, "Don't forget to turn it off." She pulled a black square box from her own pocket and flipped the switch.

They smiled at each other as though they had not been in the middle of a police roundup, but as though they were standing together, all alone, in the center of a splendid library. Which they were.

CHAPTER 40
Holy Molé!

Thomas Alfred Spalding, Elizabethan Demonology: An Essay in Illustration of the Belief in the Existence of Devils, and the Powers Possessed by Them, as it was Generally Held During the Period of the Reformation, and the Times Immediately Succeeding; with Special Reference to Shakspere [sic] and his Works, *1880, dark blue cloth with gilt on spine. Essays about what the Church of Shakespeare's time believed about devils, types of devils and angels, as well as folk beliefs about fairies and witches and how such views influence Shakespeare's plays.*

Emma stood at her work table, carefully applying a thin line of glue with a small brush to the tear between a book's front board and its spine. She finished with a deft swipe and laid the book under a sheet of waxed paper, then placed a brick wrapped in thin cloth on top. Her phone tinkled with Molly's ring.

"Hi," Molly said. "Are you busy?"

"No. What's up?" Emma glanced at the waiting stack of books and turned her back on them.

"Well, guess what? Sarah's been sentenced."

"What?"

"Jay called. Fred told Elliott that she accepted a plea bargain. She pled guilty to conspiracy on multiple charges and got a ten-year sentence."

"Will she serve the whole sentence, do you think?" Emma went into her living room and sat in her easy chair, newly upholstered. The room was almost back to normal.

"Her lawyer said she wouldn't serve more than two because the prisons are so crowded. Hey, would you like to come over? I've got some croissants from Oxygen."

"You went there without telling me!" Emma thought of Oxygen as "their place."

"Yesterday. But I planned to invite you to share them."

"Okay, I'll be there in a minute." Emma grabbed her shoulder bag, slid her feet into clogs, took a quick look in the mirror, and ran out the door. She hadn't talked to Molly since she got back from the Stratford Festival a couple of days ago. Every year she went to Stratford, Ontario, for a week to see Shakespeare plays with her friends Meredith and Darcy. It had been just what she needed, getting away from her house and bookselling, spending time with friends, absorbing some Shakespeare, leaving the whole murder investigation behind, even taking a break from Molly and how she was beginning to feel about her. But she had found herself missing Molly—her easygoing humor, her directness, her casual, relaxed manner that went side by side with her sharp, focused intellect and practical good sense. She missed Molly's blue eyes and long, rangy body. She even missed those rambunctious dogs.

At Molly's, she was surprised not to be greeted by the call and response barking she was used to.

"They're out back," Molly explained. "Barking at the trifecta."

"Tri—?"

"A boy on his bike, a stroller, and a dog. All things to be barked at."

Seated at Molly's dining room table, which was piled up like Emma's except it had more books and paraphernalia on it, she took a bite of almond croissant. "Delicious!" she said, following the bite with a swallow of tea.

She heard a commotion and scrambling from the dog door, and two eager dogs, tongues out and panting, tails wagging, surrounded her. Blavatsky's tail was making its signature windmill circles as she nosed Emma's arm, and Dmitri pawed along her shin, scratching her ankle. "Down!" Emma shouted, holding her croissant above her head.

"Don't yell," Molly said. "Just say "down" and snap your fingers."

"Down?" said Emma, trying to snap her fingers and not succeeding. Dmitri rested both paws on her lap and raising his head, sniffed toward the croissant. He smelled of leaves and his usual dog smell, though not so strong. Molly had given them baths.

"Down, guys," Molly said in a soft voice. "Over here." Her fingers snapped in the direction she wanted them to go. Both dogs lay down behind Molly's chair. Turning to Emma, she said, "I know how to get you over here, don't I? Almond croissants."

"News," Emma said, lowering her arm and taking a bite, then licking crumbs off her fingers. "That's why I came. Well, the croissants, too." She thought, but did not say, *I missed you.*

"How was Stratford?"

"We had a blast. We saw all three parts of *Henry the Sixth*, and we followed that up with *Richard the Third*."

"That sounds like a barrel of laughs!"

"Also, *HMS Pinafore* and *My Fair Lady*."

"Welcome back to the ordinary world. Well, it looks like the book fair will have a booth missing this time." Molly carefully divided some of her larger crumbs between two plates and set them on the floor one by each side of her chair. The dogs rushed to the plates and gobbled up the crumbs.

Blavatsky approached Emma and stretched out at her feet with a hopeful look on her long face. Dmitri looked at Molly, who shook her head. He curled up and rested his nose on his paws.

Molly continued, "Fred and Sarah always had the first booth inside the door. They've been fixtures at book fairs for so long. I'll miss them. Jay said Fred was so embarrassed about the whole thing, he just wants to hide for a while. So Elliott snapped up Fred's space. And you'll get Elliott's space, same row as mine."

Emma raised the croissant toward her mouth, abruptly stopped and carefully held out a triangular bit of pastry to Dmitri. He nosed it, then took it. Emma felt impressed with how he did not let even a tooth touch her fingers. They really were nice dogs. Emma wiped her fingers on a cloth napkin that she found on the table next to a roll of Mylar.

"So how are you all dealing with Fred's leaving the book fair committee?" Emma asked.

"We're overwhelmed, having to do so much of what Fred had been doing. We always try to get people into the same booth year after year so buyers can easily find them. If I moved my booth, my Goth customers might not know where I am."

"Thanks for giving me Elliott's space." A warm feeling began to spread in Emma's chest. Dmitri poked his face close to hers. She snapped her fingers. "Down!" The dog curled up on the floor about a foot away.

Molly said, "See! You have to say it right. They'll obey if you do."

Emma wanted to ask, *How was that different than before?* But she decided not to make an issue of anything to do with the dogs.

"So what will happen to Kelly?" Emma asked.

"She's being tried as an adult for manslaughter. I imagine the jury will decide that it's self-defense. The news coverage has been making an issue of her being an attractive, blond, privileged teen involved in a witch cult."

They were both quiet. Emma remembered Kelly's pale, desperate face saying, "Da-ad?" as she was led away in handcuffs.

Emma swallowed the last of her tea. Dmitri came and sat next to her, and she stroked his long head, feeling the fine bones under the silky fur. Her hand traveled over his ears and under his chin, almost without her intending it. He gave her fingers a couple of licks. "And how about Shirley?" she asked. "Is she going to plead guilty to kidnapping, or is she going to go to trial? I wonder whether she'll go to the same prison as Sarah?"

"Ha!" Molly laughed. "They'll probably organize rival witch gangs. I pity the prison guards."

"It would make a great TV series. Glenn Close as Shirley, and who would play Sarah?"

"Yeah, Glenn Close does evil well. Hm, how about Jessica Lange? You know she was in all those 'American Horror' shows, and now she quit the series. I wouldn't have believed she could play evil until I saw that show."

"Never saw it," Emma said.

"Didn't miss much. I always felt like I needed a shower after watching." Molly sipped some tea. "Wonder what Shirley will do after she gets out of jail?"

"She'll probably write a book about her experiences and go on lecture tours."

Molly laughed again. "At five figures per talk."

"I'll bet she's a dynamic speaker. You know, there's a contingent of Candler students who feel she's being treated unfairly. They've set up a Facebook page."

"Oh, yeah? Are there a lot of them?"

"I think it's mostly students who are into magic. They have names like Willowick and Fleetfoot."

"Do you reckon they hold Circles over there?"

"Maybe in the basement of the theology library. It would be perfect—unexpected turns and crannies, old, crumbling stone steps. They also have a Meetup page. I might look and see where they're going to meet next. Just out of curiosity."

Molly chuckled. "What will become of the Circle?"

"They'll probably disband, since their principal members are in jail."

"I wonder," Molly said. She looked off into space. "Willowick and her pals may take it up."

"I hope Neil and Evan will be convicted for kidnapping and breaking and entering."

"I'm sure they will be. And burglary. There's probably something about destruction of property they can be charged with."

"I sincerely hope so," Emma said, clenching her fists. "What I wish is that they could be sentenced to hard labor until they'd paid for everything they destroyed, including my books."

"They'd be working for all eternity," Molly said gently.

"Uh-huh!" Emma's fists slowly unclenched, and she grinned. "So are you all ready for the book fair?"

"Mostly," Molly answered. "You?"

"Not really. But I price and mylar my books as soon as I buy them, so my stock is in pretty good shape. Just a few repairs to make."

"You're such a Virgo!"

Emma smiled. "And you're a typical Gemini. Flying by the seat of your pants."

"Not so!" Molly said. "I only have a dozen or so books left to price. And mylar," she added. "Well, I have a lot more to mylar that have already been priced. But it's two weeks. I have plenty of time."

Emma laughed. "You're always ready in time, though. You'll stay up all night if you have to."

"Of course," Molly said. "It would go faster if I didn't have to be on the book fair committee as well." She glanced at the door to the adjoining room.

"Oh!" exclaimed Emma. "I haven't seen your new shelves since you had them installed."

"Come and see, then." Molly jumped to her feet and led the way. "Ta-dah!" she said, waving her arm.

"Wow." Emma looked around at the newly renovated room, formerly the second bedroom in Molly's house. The shelves stretched from floor to ceiling on three walls. Emma walked slowly in, looking around. "So this is Bernard Booth's collection."

"That's right," Molly said. "I got rid of the moldy ones. Can't have them in my house."

"Are you putting any of these in your booth this year?"

"As many as I can get priced and catalogued. My list

online has already doubled."

"Not all of them, though?" Emma said, looking sidewise at Molly.

Molly met her eye. "Of course not."

"Where is it?" Emma almost whispered.

Molly went over to the middle shelf facing them. She lifted down a heavy, leather-covered book and carefully opened it.

Emma peered inside. It was a fake book with a hollow interior. Inside was some wadded-up tissue. As Emma watched, Molly removed a layer to reveal a small, plastic-wrapped book. She reverently lifted it out.

Emma raised her eyes to Molly's, and then looked back at the plastic bag.

"*A Boke of Secret Knowlege.*" She whispered the words. "*By A Learned Doctor.*"

Molly gave a small chuckle. Carefully, she lifted one thin, brittle page after another until she reached the place where a smaller sheet had been laid in.

Emma read aloud, "*Whosoever . . .*"

Molly lifted the smaller, laid-in sheet. The demon's face glared at them with tongue stuck out, ears sticking up like a donkey's, tusks curling around its lips. Molly covered it with the smaller sheet. "Ephemera united with its book," she said with satisfaction. She closed the book, replaced it under the wadded tissue, closed the fake book, and replaced it on the shelf.

They didn't say anything for a moment. Molly said, "You know, I'm a little leery about it. I might get a safety deposit box. What if some Circle member breaks in? They know I bought the collection, and they're bound to realize at some point that I have their sacred text."

"I have an idea," Emma said. "What if you donate it to Candler's Special Collections?"

Molly looked askance. "I dunno—"

"We can visit it whenever we want. And it'll be publicized to warn Willowick and friends from breaking in."

Molly still looked reluctant.

"And anyone who wants to look at it will have a security guard standing over them."

"Ha! They'll need to have a criminal background check before looking at it."

They laughed, walking back to the dining room. Molly said, "You know, I've changed my thinking a little about magic—or capital M Magic."

"How have you changed?"

"I think it may not be so innocent after all to try to bend events to your will with it, even if it doesn't have much reality."

"Do you think it has any?" asked Emma.

"Mmmm, maybe. I mean, I don't know if Bernard Booth's spell really made that car go off the road and burst into flames. But Shirley believed it did. And moreover, she was willing to have it done for her. That's more disturbing to me, that she would accept it and the benefits it brought her."

Emma nodded. "The evil comes from within human beings?"

"Exactly. The willingness to do such a thing, whether you can actually bend the laws of nature or not."

"The Renaissance ceremonial magicians, like Simon Forman, didn't worship the devil, although they did try to summon demons. And angels," Emma added. "I don't think that the Circle worships the devil either, even if they did have that inverted pentagram. But they are willing—at least Bernard was willing—to use whatever powers there are to benefit themselves even if that involves harming others." Emma spoke slowly, following her thoughts carefully.

"That's where I draw the line," Molly said.

"So you accept White Magic."

"I accept the possibility," Molly said. Her blue eyes looked into Emma's.

Emma felt her body turn warm. *Those eyes*, she thought. She turned away, squinting at the spines of the books. "That's okay, then. The moralist in me doesn't object to your accepting the possibility." She wanted to go home to finish mending, but she also wanted to linger here with Molly.

Molly said, "Would you like to try a new place tonight for dinner? And we don't have to talk about murder or murderous witches."

"Sure. Where?" *Was this a date?*

"It's Mexican. Holy Molé."

"I've heard of it, but haven't been there yet."

"You like margaritas?" Those blue eyes were hoping for the right answer.

"Sure. It's not too pricey, is it?"

"No. And even better, tonight is $5.00 margaritas!"

"Yes," Emma said softly. "I'd like that very much."

Molly beamed. "Shall I pick you up at 7:00?"

Emma nodded. "Okay." She looked down. "And, Molly..." she hesitated.

"What?" Molly's smile dropped away, leaving her looking worried.

"Oh, nothing." Emma started to turn away. Then she turned back. "Molly, I want you to know that—I really like going places with you. I—I hope we can get together more." She felt her heart thumping.

Molly looked surprised. Then she smiled again, a warm smile that made Emma feel tingly all over. "Yeah," she said. "I really like going places with you too."

Emma wanted to say more, but she felt, looking up at Molly, that for the moment, this was enough.

About the Author

Charlene Ball is the author of the award-winning DARK LADY: A NOVEL OF EMILIA BASSANO LANYER (She Writes Press, 2017). She has a lifelong love of the Renaissance and its literature and history. She has taught English and Women's Studies. In 2009 she retired from the Institute for Women's, Gender, and Sexuality Studies at Georgia State University. Since retirement, she has been busier than ever with writing, volunteer work, and bookselling. She is a member of the Atlanta Writers Club and the Georgia Writers Association and a fellow of the Hambidge Center for Creative Arts and Sciences. She is married to author and bookseller Libby Ware. They collaborate on writing bibliomysteries under the name of Lily Charles. MURDER AT THE ESTATE SALE is their first collaboration and the first in the Molly and Emma Booksellers series.

Libby Ware is the author of the award-winning LUM: A NOVEL, published in 2015. She is the owner of Toadlily Books, an antiquarian book business. She is president of the Georgia Antiquarian Booksellers Association, and is a member of the Antiquarian Booksellers Association of America, the International League of Booksellers, Atlanta Writers Club and the Georgia Writers Association. She is a fellow of the Hambidge Center for Creative Arts and Sciences. Libby lives in Atlanta with her dog Robin about a mile from her wife Charlene Ball. They collaborate on writing bibliomysteries under the name of Lily Charles. MURDER AT THE ESTATE SALE is their first bibliomystery and the first in the Molly and Emma Booksellers series.

www.ingramcontent.com/pod-product-compliance
Lightning Source LLC
LaVergne TN
LVHW011812060526
838200LV00053B/3754